HOW DOES OUR LORD FEEL

ABOUT CHRISTMAS TODAY?

SCOTT RANKIN

Self-Published

Self-Published, Printed in Ponder, Texas - United States of America
ISBN 978-1-7340848-0-1
Library of Congress Control Number: 2019918294

Edited by Write My Wrongs Editing

Special thanks to Rachelle Rankin, Nate Moore, Melissa Russell, and Kevin & Laurie Brannen for their valuable contributions

Book Cover Design was created through 99designs.com – Cover Design by designer IR Graphics

Typesetter Kara Rankin

All scripture quotations are taken from the WEB version with some *(italics in parenthesis)* added by the author for clarification.

Publisher's Cataloging-In-Publication Data
(Prepared by The Donohue Group, Inc.)

Names: Rankin, Scott, 1972- author.
Title: The Christian Christmas condition : how does the Lord feel about Christmas today? / Scott Rankin.
Description: [Ponder, Texas] : Scott Rankin, [2019] | Series: [The Christian condition series] | Includes bibliographical references.
Identifiers: ISBN 9781734084801 | ISBN 9781734084818 (ebook)
Subjects: LCSH: Christian life--21st century. | Christmas--Religious aspects--Christianity--21st century. | Christmas--Social aspects--21st Century. | Word of God. | Jesus Christ.
Classification: LCC BV4597.23 .R36 2019 (print) | LCC BV4597.23 (ebook) | DDC 248.4--dc23

This Book is Dedicated To:

The woman and writer I most admire

who listens for the voice of God

to compose inspiration from her soul

with elegance, splendor and a creativity

stirring all who bask in her thoughts.

I can only aspire to write as well.

She has further taught me

by her living example,

honesty is key,

serve others,

question everything, and

always expect good things from God.

She is a precious and valuable vessel from the Lord

Rachelle

Acknowledgment & Special Thanks

To find the right cover images that would accurately convey the message inside this book, I went searching for a face of Jesus that could represent the gentle and humble nature of our Lord as described in Matthew 11:28-30. My first request for permission to use a painting I thought might work, was denied. My spirits immediately were dampened, discouraged I might have to settle for something less than perfect.

But, when I stumbled on the image of Jesus' face you see on the front cover, I knew it would accomplish my goal flawlessly. The painting was so good though, I worried that obtaining permission to use might be out of reach. I tried anyway and sent off my request to the painter, Russ Docken. The response I received was unexpected.

It was such a wonderful experience to find not only a painting that vividly captured the essence of a Savior who loves us despite the messes we constantly get ourselves into… but also to discover that the artist, in dealing with my urgent request, exhibited the very same qualities of humbleness and generosity as the subject he chose to paint.

As an expression of my thankfulness to Mr. Russ Docken for his quick consideration, generosity, and help when I was in a difficult position and a time crunch, I want to recognize him and invite you to explore the exquisite art of this extremely talented and humble man at RussDockenOriginals.com

Thank you Russ!
-Scott Rankin

Thank you for reading *The Christian Christmas Condition.*

Follow author Scott Rankin and be the first to know about upcoming early book releases, sneak peeks, FREE or DISCOUNTED deals, blog tour information, and other great BONUS materials!

Sign up here:

https://www.scottrankin.com/bonus

INTRODUCTION

As the Christmas season approaches, we can all expect to see pine trees covered with brightly colored bulbs, people dressed in Santa Claus suits ringing bells outside store entrances, and houses outlined in beautifully orchestrated tiny lights. Joy seems to be dancing in the air, painted on our faces, and flashing like sparkles on our outer winter wear. But for those of us who are willing to look for it, we can also detect some less desirable Christmas trends, like unwanted stress, a needless pressure to rush, or perhaps greed and extravagance.

Even as Christians, our focus can slowly be drawn away from Jesus, and we start to lose sight of "whose" we are and what He wants us to be during this season: ambassadors expected to spread the good news of Christ along with our good tidings of cheer.

Most of us can look back over the years and easily say, "Christmas is not what it used to be." Although we know technological advances and evolving traditions contribute to ever-changing times, that should never be an excuse, reason, or justification for us to veer off course from God's values and miss what is truly important.

This introduces the valid topic of our discussion: who is Christmas really for? What is happening with Christmas these days and through time? And most importantly, what in the world are we as Christians supposed to do with it all? While some people want us to avoid Christmas because it may promote commercialism and foster selfishness in many, others want to "save Christmas" because it provides a rare opportunity to share Christ with others and worship Him, too. As Christians, how are we to handle this toss-up situation?

While we progress through this study together, two important truths will serve as our foundation. First, for all that Christ has done for us, He needs to be honored. Jesus is Lord, and the Son of God. He came to rescue us from an eternity of punishment for our own sins by offering us complete eternal redemption if we choose to believe in Him (John 3:16). When all is said and done, Jesus needs to be honored in a way that honors God (even during the Christmas season). Second, the Bible must be the final authority on all choices we make when navigating through life because the Bible is the written word of both God and Jesus. Two scriptures establish this fact: John 1:1-18 and 2 Timothy 3:16-17.

When considering options on almost any decision we're going to make, we draw from or receive information, advice, and influences from many different sources. While all these influences can sway us in various directions, God's word needs to be the anchor that keeps us steady amidst all that tosses our analyzing minds back and forth. We should never compromise God's instructions, examples, or desires in favor of our own opinions, or of the advice of movie stars, famous people, politicians, family, social media, or even other good preachers. In the end, God and His Word must be the pillar of final authority upon which all our decisions are hinged.

However, the Bible cannot help you navigate if you are not familiar with what it says. No matter the issue or problem we face, Christians (those who follow Christ where He leads) should have a habit of going to God first before making any decisions. So, let's take that same approach here in this study. We will:

1. Go to God first in His Word.
2. Ask ourselves, *Is there anything in His written word about this topic? Are there any examples given on this topic?* We need to read and meditate on these to find God's desire.
3. Ask God for the discernment of the Holy Spirit for guidance.
4. Listen for His voice to distinguish His truth from our own understanding and weed out any of Satan's possible influences.
5. Follow our shepherd if the truths that He reveals lead us to a different path than that of our own opinions.

As we progress through this study together, I recommend you use your Bible frequently rather than take my views as gospel truth. God's Word is the living spoken truth that always guides us in the direction He wants us to go. The discussion in this book will address different positions about Christmas, the Christmas tree, Santa Claus, Christmas traditions, and what this holiday celebration is meant to be from the perspective of a follower of Christ.

Although this book may delve into Christmas topics and traditions, its definitive purpose is to teach, encourage, and empower you to employ the techniques of studying the Word, then calling on, listening for, and following the leading of the Holy Spirit in every future topic, problem, or situation you will face. This will help you more easily recognize and act upon God's planned direction for you… not just at Christmas, but all year long.

CONTENTS

- CHAPTER 1 -

"TOP 10" LIST

Merry Christmas! Put your holiday thinking caps on, because we're warming up with two fun challenges. First, I'm going to give you three sets of lyrics. Your job is to see how much of each song you can remember. If you feel like singing out loud, be my guest. Ready?

1. Oh, you better watch out, you better not…
2. Rudolph the…
3. I'm dreaming of a…

Now, let's get into the Christmas spirit with our final exercise: when I say "go," quickly list the top ten things you associate with the Christmas season. You may include past memories or present-day traditions; anything related to Christmas, and there are no wrong answers. This exercise is about the first things that pop into your mind, so complete your list as quickly as you can. You can use the space provided below or get your own sheet of paper, but please don't skip this brief exercise, as you'll want to reference your list later!

When you're done, we'll continue on the next page. Ready… Set… Go!

Here are a few popular answers: Jingle Bells, cutting out paper snowflakes, snowball fights, writing letters to Santa Claus, vacation from school, mistletoe, sitting by a warm fireplace on a cold night, trimming the Christmas tree, hanging stockings, setting out cookies and milk for Santa Claus, candlelight mass, Christmas lights on houses, and family reunions… Some of our fondest memories circulate around this time of year!

I once asked a woman named Lisa to do this exercise out loud, and she did an amazing job of listing a large number of family-related activities. However, not one thing she listed had any correlation with Jesus, His birth, worship, angels announcing Jesus' birth, or a manger scene. Now, Lisa loves the Lord, but I asked her why she had so many other thoughts come to mind before Jesus—and her answer unveiled the perfect premise for this book (thank you, Lisa). She said, "I guess we're all just conditioned to think that way." So now I ask, if we've really been conditioned… what condition are Christians in during Christmas?

What did your top ten list look like? Did Jesus make the cut? Now, let's add another layer to this "top 10" list exercise. When you see your kids or any immediate family member today, ask them to take the same challenge. Their answers may astonish you (partly because they do not have the chance to read the introduction of this book beforehand). Their responses should be wonderfully raw.

As you compare other people's responses, where did Jesus get put in the order? Was He first? Was He in the middle? Was He in the back? Or was He left out altogether? If you found anywhere through the results of your own experiment that Jesus did not dominate or top your list, or those of your friends and family members, then let's examine why together.

You will find that there are a variety of different views among people about Christmas and its traditions. We've all heard phrases like:

- "Jesus… the reason for the season"
- "Let's put Christ back into Christmas"
- "We need to save Christmas"
- "Happy Holidays" (instead of "Merry Christmas")

Some in the body of Christ regard Christmas as a pagan holiday, believing we should not observe it at all. Many contend that Christmas was created to honor baby Jesus and it's very important to keep this tradition so we can worship Him. Others still will point out that Christmas has now become so commercialized that we just need to get back to what is really important.

So, what is the real reason for the Christmas season? How did Christmas celebrations begin? How does God want us to use Christmas to worship and honor His Son? These are some great questions, and that is what we are going to cover in this book.

When Lisa suggested so appropriately that we have been "conditioned," it simply implies that your surroundings, history, and family traditions have trained you to think a certain way. Truth be told, you were probably born into family traditions and influenced greatly as a child by your surroundings to put presents, the Christmas tree, or Santa first, all the while letting God and Jesus share the spotlight every now and then. In doing so, you may find that Jesus, over time, inadvertently moved out of the first priority position because of conditioned habits during this season.

But don't lose heart—conditioned does not mean permanent. God tells us that through Him, we can renew our minds! And with a renewed mind comes an overflow of blessings.

So, sit back and enjoy while we study "The Christian Christmas Condition."

- CHAPTER 2 -

WHAT DO YOU THINK?

Making life decisions with the Bible as your moral compass causes your life to be different FROM the world, and look different TO the world. We are called to "love our neighbor" and be the "light" in a dark world for a reason. His love and His light create a beautifully unique attraction in us for the purpose of drawing the world to Him.

So, as followers (ambassadors) of Jesus Christ, our Christmas-time habits and celebration methods should LOOK different than those of a non-believer. We shouldn't be trying so hard to blend in or look the same as the world. It is the differences in your life that can spark others to ask you the questions, "Why do you have so much joy?" or "Why do things go so well for you?" We want people to pick up on those differences in our lives and react to them with curiosity. When they genuinely inquire why, your natural response can introduce them to all the benefits and the goodness of God (Psalm 103:2; Psalm 118:17). Therefore, it truly is the differences in your life that can make a difference in the world!

If your life, including your Christmas traditions, looks the same as everybody else's, nobody is going to be asking questions. If there are no questions asked, then there can be no response from you about the goodness of God. It's a sad condition to be in if a Christian's life is making little to no impact for Christ. What condition do you want to be in?

So, what is the condition of Christians today during Christmas? I'd like for us to really examine Christmas and go deeper into its meaning so we can understand how it's supposed to look for a Christian. To do that, let's start with a set of warm-up questions. What are your answers to the following?

1. Are we getting all that Christmas has in store for us?
2. Are our most cherished memories generated from what we received… or what we gave?
3. Is our attitude supposed to be "what can Christmas give us?" or should it be "what can we give God through Christmas?"
4. Is Christmas fundamentally supposed to be worship to God, or is it just a time of joy and goodwill for all? Could it be both?

5. What was Christmas originally instituted to be?
6. Was Christmas created by God for us? Created by us for God? Or was Christmas created by God for Jesus?
7. Can some Christmas traditions potentially lead us away from God if we're not careful?

How would your answers compare to your friends or relatives? How would your answers compare to someone who may not be a follower of Christ? Those were some basic warm-up questions that barely scratch the surface of this topic. You may have come up with some excellent thoughts and great opinions in your answers, but what I want you to do now is table all those great answers and thoughts in order to come back and discuss them later. Set them aside in a pile on an imaginary table and label it, "What I think about Christmas."

Now consider this: all those questions were geared to pull knowledge, opinions, and feelings directly from you. They were rooted in, "What do YOU think?" But, when compared to what God says, what YOU think does not matter at all, because your opinions do not establish absolute truth. God establishes truth. Therefore, the only thing that really matters is what God thinks and what He tells us! When Jesus was in the wilderness at the end of His temptation, He told Satan, "Man shall not live by bread alone, but by every word that proceeds out of the mouth of God" (Matt. 4:4). Since Jesus knew that His survival depended upon every word that comes from the mouth of God, and since Christians are to be "Christ-like," then at the very base of Christianity, we lay aside our own opinions and follow what God tells us to do with the intention of not only surviving but being transformed into the likeness of Christ.

If our Christian walk truly is inspired by our desire to become more like Christ, shouldn't we be asking ourselves how He would have us celebrate the Christmas holiday?

- CHAPTER 3 -

WHAT DOES GOD THINK?

In the previous chapter, a few of the starter questions we considered were about how to best worship God during Christmas. However, all of those were centered around what we as humans think. But I contend that for true "followers" of Christ (those who diligently want to follow God's lead at all costs), these next three questions may be a much deeper, more challenging, and more meaningful place to start when considering the importance of placing Christ in the best place possible within our minds, hearts, and habits, in order to honor Him the way He wants to be honored during this holiday season. Instead of being human-centered, like the previous questions, the following questions are God-centered.

The following are three big questions, and I'd like you to spend at least sixty seconds on each one, developing more than just a quick one-word or one-thought answer. Think hard, grow much. Are you ready?

1. Does God specifically say or request anything in the Bible about any Christmas traditions we participate in today? If so, where do we see this in the Bible (specific book, chapter, verse, or just generic Old Testament or New Testament)?
2. Did God institute a holiday to worship the birth of His son, Jesus? If so, give the approximate reference(s).
3. Finally, the biggest question of all: am I willing to follow the voice and leading of my Shepherd in any certain area, even if it might bring possible embarrassment from family, friends, or neighbors, in order to honor God's desires?

These are three tough questions, but once we know and are grounded in the answers to these three God-centered questions, then the answers to all other questions about Christmas easily fall into place. Before we continue, I want to go ahead and give you a little teaser. Do you remember the first activity I asked you to do when you started? I shared with you a list of holiday memories that popped in my head, many of which were longstanding and generational traditions in my family that helped create a great deal of my most cherished and joyful Christmastime memories.

When my wife and I started studying these three God-centered questions and found out God actually addresses today's holiday traditions, even telling us the way He wants to be worshipped, my family changed a few of the ways we celebrate the goodness of God, Jesus, and Jesus' birth during December. This resulted in our minds being opened, redirected, or "renewed," if you will, to a new and refreshing way of seeing Christmas. A God-centered mentality now has our family moving away from a few of the things the world has conditioned us to think and do, and we feel like we are being swept through giant doors into a God kingdom mindset where we are now enjoying a "Christmas spirit" all year round. Although it may look a little different from typical families and traditions, this approach is definitely much more rewarding!

By redefining your "Christmas spirit," it's my hope that you can enjoy new and exciting blessings God has in store for you and your family all year long and pass the same blessings down to your future generations for many years to come!

You may have a trove of wonderful family Christmas memories in the past. It is not my intention to rob or steal away any Christmas tradition memories you cherish. No! Keep those gems of joy, laughter, and togetherness with you in your mind. Rather, it is my intention to offer a proverbial "treasure map" that, should you choose to seek the treasure, may require a choice on your part to let go of something small—something you've held in your hand for a lifetime—in order to wrap your arms around something much bigger and newer from God. It will change you, your children, your grandchildren, and your continuing generations forever… for the better! Ultimately, the decision is entirely yours. Are you curious?

Look at the last of our three God-centered questions: am I willing at all cost to honor God's requests in any area (even if it means embarrassment from neighbors, friends, and/or family members)? The answer to this question lies within the story of a familiar Bible character. Our study, our quest, begins with Gideon!

- CHAPTER 4 -

GIDEON: HERO OR ROLE MODEL

Are you familiar with the story of Gideon? In the sixth chapter of book of Judges, God's people had been suffering harassment from a neighboring country for seven years. Gideon was tired of and frustrated by this oppression. He also felt weak and insignificant as a person, yet, with God's encouragement and instruction, he took only 300 Israelites into battle and defeated 120,000 Midianites to rescue God's people. This is a ratio of one good guy to every 400 bad guys, and the good guys won the battle using clay pots, torches, and trumpets… and, of course, God's miraculous help! If you're not familiar with the details of this monumental battle story, please read Judges, chapters six, seven, and eight before moving on.

God does astonishing things through those who may feel or deem themselves weak or insignificant. Some people might ask, "Can God do amazing things with me like He did with Gideon?" Of course He can! As evidenced throughout the Bible, including Acts (10:34-35) and James (5:17), God is no respecter of persons and often uses ordinary, everyday people to spark great change. God can do great things through you if you submit yourself to His leading.

Gideon is a great example of an average person who God raised to greatness, but let's examine a part of his story that many of our Sunday school teachers and preachers leave out. Let's go back to the beginning of the story, in Judges chapter six. Here we find Gideon threshing wheat in a winepress to hide from the Midianites who had been stealing food from and oppressing God's people for seven years. An angel of the Lord (manifestation of the Lord Himself) appears to Gideon (Judges 6:16) and proclaims Gideon will lead His people into battle and save His people from the Midianites. God encourages and edifies Gideon, and, as a sign of validation, the angel of God performs a miracle right before Gideon's eyes by burning up a food offering he had prepared for the angel of the Lord.

Just having a conversation with the angel of God and witnessing the miracle would be an extremely incredible experience for anyone… I know it would be for me. But watch what happens next. That same night, God shows up and asks Gideon to put it all on the line. He asks him to tear down the Altar of Baal, which was located right in the center of town, and tear down the Asherah pole beside it. He was then to build a proper altar to the only true God and worship Him by sacrificing his own father's bull (Judges 6:25-26).

It is important to know this altar of Baal is in the middle of the community where everyone in town has grown accustomed to worshipping Baal. We also know it was significantly important to the people of his town, because Gideon was afraid to tear it down in the daytime where everyone could see him do it! In fact, they even threatened to kill him after the task was completed.

You might ask, what is an Asherah pole? An Asherah pole is a sacred tree or pole that was erected near Canaanite worship sites or brought into the home in order to glorify their mother-goddess Asherah (also known as Astarte). She was considered the fertility goddess and procreation mate of El and Baal, the supreme gods of pagan Canaanite religion. One of the ways to give Asherah glory and honor, was to place gifts or presents at the base of her pole or tree.

We must understand that Gideon was born into these traditions, and thus, he was "conditioned" from birth to think it was okay to have these worship tools in the middle of his town and to participate in or tolerate the use of them. Gideon was from the tribe of Benjamin which still acknowledged the God of Abraham, Isaac, and Jacob to some extent, even though some divided their worship between the Lord and other Canaanite gods. These mixed rituals, family history, and patterns of duel worship were all Gideon knew from birth, until God revealed Himself and gave Gideon a new view of truth, a new way to worship, and tradition toward the God of Israel. By the way, truth—*real* truth—is God's reality revealed to us. Gideon was getting a firsthand dose of truth on how to worship God.

This new truth revealed a pure way of worshipping God; it was a form of worship free of man-made traditions! It was more holy, honoring, and pleasing to God. It was what God desired from His people. Most importantly, it was what God told Gideon to do. And at this point in the story, the blessings in store for Gideon, his home town, and all of God's nation were right around the corner of obedience. Gideon's obedience to remove man's rituals and traditions that offended God was the key. Take notice: the historic miracle battle that made Gideon famous did not happen until after Gideon obeyed, honored, and worshipped God. This paved the way for God to usher in and deliver the victory and recognition Gideon would later receive. There is a distinct pattern to observe.

First, God is asking Gideon to remove a manmade tradition (from Gideon's perspective, this was the Altar of Baal and the Asherah pole), even in the face of guaranteed embarrassment and possible persecution and/or death by his own townspeople. Second, God wants to be honored through obedience and worship (sacrificing the bull on God's altar, not Baal's) before He blesses Gideon and uses him to do a mighty work through a miracle battle to rescue God's people—which happens a few days later in the story.

Can you see the pattern?

1. REMOVE manmade traditions hated by God, even in the face of persecution and/or danger
2. HONOR God through obedience and WORSHIP or faith
3. God rewards the obedience and honor by performing a MIRACLE or great work, often through the servant

The point I'm trying to make through this story of Gideon is that blessings, honor, and recognition for the Bible hero don't just appear out of thin air. They follow faith, obedience, and worship. A similar pattern is seen in so many other Bible leaders: Noah, Abraham, Isaac, Jacob, Joseph, Moses, Joshua, all the heroes in the book of Judges, David, Jehoshaphat, all the prophets, Zacharias, Mary, Jesus, the Apostles, Paul. And it doesn't stop there. By applying this pattern today, any one of us can behave exactly like these Bible characters. To do this, though, we must transform our vision from looking at these characters as untouchable heroes to seeing them as humans just like us who handle tough situations with tough faith and obedience. Then, in making them our role models, we can follow their lead. There is nothing special about any of these humans (yes, even Jesus was human—he just relied on His Father far better than anyone else) except that they were willing to make hard choices to honor God in their thinking and behavior through tough situations. The choices they made are not at all out of our reach.

As it relates to us today, when we sow seeds of faith, obedience, and worship into God, He lifts us up with blessings and sometimes executes great 'Gideon-type' miracles that we get to be a part of. Gideon can be your hero figure, where you separate yourself, stand back, and say, "Wow, Gideon sure had to have a lot of trust in God! I can only admire him because I'd never be able to do what he did!" Or, Gideon can be your role model, where you directly connect with him and say, "If God is no respecter of persons, then He can use me in a mighty way today—just like He did with Gideon!"

So I now throw this back in your lap: is Gideon just going to be your faraway, up-on-the-bookshelf hero to whom you merely look with admiration, or is Gideon going to be your role model who serves as your inspiration to follow, honor, and worship God with courage?

- CHAPTER 5 -

CURIOSITY KILLS THE SACRED COW

Why is Gideon's story so important? It's because Gideon's situation is so very close in resemblance to what many Christians are experiencing today. Gideon's response to a request from a holy God to renounce tradition resulted in blessings and miracles beyond imagination. I have found that when I respond to God in the same way, I too have received more miracles and blessings in my life than I can count, and that's what I want for you. That's the reason I'm sharing this with you today.

For a moment, I'd like to do a little bit of role play... I would like to put you in Gideon's shoes. If you were Gideon, and God Himself came down today and asked you to tear down the city's altar to Baal along with the Asherah pole, and to sacrifice your father's bull in order to worship Him, would you do it? Would you be afraid, like Gideon was?

Are you going to delay God's plan by first choosing to weigh out the consequences? "Hold on, God, you're telling me you want me to go tear down the altar… and the Asherah pole… *and* sacrifice Dad's sacred bull? Wait a minute—what assurances do I have that I'm gonna come out of this thing alive? And what's in it for me?"

Would it make your decision easier to follow through with if God told you ahead of time that the altar and pole were both an abomination to Him? If you knew how much God despised the worshipping of false gods, would that help motivate you more to get rid of the idols?

I understand it's difficult to imagine tearing down someone else's property. But what if you were the owner? That's right, you own the pole, the altar, and even the cow. Does that make the task easier? How fast would you tear it down if it all belonged to you *and* it was in your house?

I'm asking you to put yourself in Gideon's shoes because God has already talked to you, and to me, to show us some of today's Christmas traditions that are displeasing Him in the very same manner that Gideon's homeland worship traditions were displeasing Him. Are you curious to know exactly which traditions I'm talking about? Are you curious to know where and how God addresses today's Christmas traditions in the Bible? Good! I want you to grab your Bible and hang on tight, because that curiosity for what God has already said may just help us to kill a few sacred cows!

- CHAPTER 6 -

IDOLS ARE CONDEMNED BY GOD

Grab your shovels and your Bibles, 'cause we're going diggin' deep into the word of God. Let's bring back the first God-centered question from earlier: Does God specifically say or request anything in the Bible about Christmas traditions we participate in today, and where in the Bible would we find this information?

Now, keep in mind, the word "Christmas" is never used in the Bible. You'll never hear the Bible say "Thou shalt not celebrate Christmas," and you certainly won't read, "Behold, unto thee is born a savior, and I give thee Christmas to celebrate His birth." Christmas cannot directly be condemned or even be supported in the Bible by using this exact word, "Christmas." However, by collectively combining four puzzle pieces with scripture and a good understanding of history, we find that God specifically addresses our question above in Jeremiah, Exodus, Deuteronomy, Hosea, and Romans. Not only does God address it, but His position is unarguably crystal-clear.

I predict that in the next five chapters, you're going to think, or maybe even say aloud, "Wow! I never knew the Bible said that!" Let's take a careful look at these four elements, then piece them together to discover a very surprising truth. Open your Bible to Jeremiah chapter ten and follow along with me to discover exactly what God says, verse by verse.

SEEKING PUZZLE PIECE #1:

In Jeremiah 10, around 627 B.C., after Israelites had been living in the Promised Land for a while and were surrounded by sinful nations, we read in verse 1, "Hear the word which Yahweh speaks to you, house of Israel!"

Now, keep in mind, God is not just speaking to the Israelites of that day! He's talking to you and me, and here's my reasoning: The command given by God in the next four verses *will not* cease to be effective in the next generation that follows. What I mean is, God will not say, "Listen up my people. It's now 627 B.C, but when your next sons are born, I want you to forget everything I'm about to tell you!" Certainly not! This next message will be just as personal to their sons, grandsons, great-grandsons, etc. This generational chain will take us up to the death of

Jesus, but it won't stop there. Because Galatians chapter 3 proves you and I are the Seed of Abraham through our faith in Christ Jesus, we are a part of the continued generations of God's people... the same ones who are being addressed by God in Jeremiah. No matter what, there is no getting around the fact that what we are about to read in Jeremiah is actually spoken toward you and me today!

God continues in verse 2 with, "Don't learn the way of the nations, and don't be dismayed at the signs of the sky; for the nations are dismayed at them." Here, God is setting us up to avoid heathen traditions, saying, "DO NOT learn the way of the Gentiles. DO NOT be dismayed at the signs of heaven..." Signs of heaven? What is He talking about? This means don't practice astrology using zodiac signs, alignment of the planets, horoscopes, and other such practices to persuade or dictate your decisions or future actions.

Verse 3 says, "For the customs of the peoples are vanity; for one cuts a tree out of the forest, the work of the hands of the workman with the ax." In the first phrase here, God says the customs or traditions of these people are futile, useless, pointless, fruitless, unsuccessful, vain, ineffective, wasted. Next, He gives us a good example of wasted time, describing a particular custom in detail. He says, "one cuts a tree out of the forest..." Now, look at verse 4!

The Bible says, "They deck it with silver and with gold; they fasten it with nails and with hammers, that it not move" (Jeremiah 10:4). I want to suggest that this description represents a tree cut down from the forest, with all branches removed. The trunk is cut or carved, shaped, completely covered or inlaid with gold and/or silver, fastened at the base so the manmade, wooden "god" doesn't fall over (because it would be very embarrassing for any particular god to fall over while being bowed to because his creators forgot to nail his feet to the floor). We might think of this image as a totem pole, but it is most definitely a *tool* used for worshipping the gods of heathen nations.

Then, in verse 5, God tells us, "They are like a palm tree, of turned work, and don't speak: they must be carried, because they can't go. Don't be afraid of them; for they can't do evil, neither is it in them to do good." God is clear. These idols can't talk, move on their own, or do either good or bad things for people. Don't be afraid of them.

Now, let's jump backward in our Bibles to Exodus 20:4-6. Here we read the second commandment from the Ten Commandments: "(4) You shall not make for yourselves an idol, nor any image of anything that is in the heavens above, or that is in the earth beneath, or that is in the water under the earth: (5) you shall not bow yourself down to them, nor serve them, for I, Yahweh your God, am a jealous God, visiting the iniquity of the fathers on the children, on the third and on the fourth generation of those who hate me, (6) and showing loving kindness to thousands of those who love me and keep my commandments." The primary focus here is God's absolute hatred for idols. But please don't miss the strong and obvious promise of God's loving kindness that will be shown for those who avoid idols!

What we draw out of Jeremiah and the Ten Commandments is this: do not make idols, do not use idols, do not trust in idols, and do not fear the idols of your enemies. Idols are inanimate objects cut by men, carried by men, carved and decorated by men, and erected by men. Idols cannot think; idols cannot speak, walk, or do anything for themselves. If your enemies pray that the idol bring evil or destruction over you, the idol cannot do evil. If your enemies ask the idol to bless them with good weather, crops, or victories in battle, the idol cannot deliver good things. The idols cannot do good, and they cannot do bad; they cannot do anything. Idols are simply tools used to inculcate trust *in* a particular god and funnel worship *toward* a particular god.

PUZZLE PIECE #1:

And so, we have now established our first piece of the puzzle: GOD HATES IDOLS. Our God commands us not to have anything to do with idols… IDOLS ARE CONDEMNED BY GOD.

- CHAPTER 7 -

A TOOL FOR WORSHIP

Now that we have our first piece of the puzzle, turn in your Bible to Hosea 4:5-6, which reads, "… so you will stumble by day, and the prophet also will stumble with you by night… (6) My people are destroyed for a lack of knowledge. Because you have rejected knowledge, I will also reject you…"

What Hosea is saying here is this: when you purposefully turn a blind eye or reject the knowledge of God, it *can* destroy you. As Christians, sometimes we don't have all the answers, but that's never an excuse to avoid seeking knowledge… or reject it! These three verses highlight God's advising for us to seek knowledge:

- Proverbs 18:15 says, "The heart of the discerning gets knowledge. The ear of the wise seeks knowledge."

- Proverbs 15:14, "The heart of one who has understanding seeks knowledge."
- 2 Peter 1:5, "Yes, and for this very cause adding on your part all diligence, in your faith supply moral excellence; and in moral excellence, knowledge"

Seeking knowledge can bring us the answers we need to move ourselves closer to God and closer to the kingdom life He intends for us.

With that, let's look for knowledge about the history of Christmas and the Christmas tree to help us make a wise decision.

SEEKING PUZZLE PIECE #2:

A Google search of "history of the Christmas tree" should provide a plethora of material to study. In short, we don't have a precise date of exactly when or how the Christmas tree tradition was born, but we do know how it developed over time. Here's a brief timeline synopsis of the development of Christmas and the use of a Christmas tree, all starting before Jesus was born:

2000 – 100 B.C.

Stories of the tree's beginnings vary, but all commonalities point to this: long before Christ's birth, history shows different forms of evergreen trees, bushes, or green wreaths being used across multiple nations in homes during winter solstice celebrations, which fall between December 21 – 22 and mark the shortest day of the year. Throughout the world, this celebration with evergreens (representing flourishing life) signified the return of longer days and more sunshine by means of a culture's particular god. In various countries, it was also believed that evergreens would ward off witches, ghosts, evil spirits, and illness. Using these evergreens, Egyptians worshipped the god called Ra, Canaanites worshipped Baal and Asherah, Romans worshipped Saturnalia, the god of agriculture, Vikings of Scandinavia worshipped their sun god, Balder, and Germans worshipped Thor, just to name a few.

Early A.D.

There is no recorded celebration of Christmas yet, but there is an annual winter festival observed throughout the Roman world. At the time of winter solstice in Rome, Saturnalia was the most significant festive event in Roman Life. It was a lawless, week-long festival observed December 17 through December 25, during which no person could be arrested or convicted for harming or murdering people, raping, stealing, or committing any other crime, usually. Other merriment also included drinking, orgies, running naked in the streets, and many other behaviors that would certainly not honor God. Although many people took advantage of the lawlessness, Saturnalia could also be a time of compassion and benevolence. Throughout Saturnalia, many Romans participated in jollity and gift-giving. But whether a culture relied on the evergreens, the lawlessness, or the compassionate gift-giving, these were all tools used to worship and honor someone else's particular god.

0 – 30 A.D.

Neither the Bible nor Jesus Himself ever mentions His day of birth. This time introduces the ministry of Jesus, and even while He is alive, there is no record of Him or His disciples (either in Christian writings or secular documentations) ever celebrating His birthday. After His crucifixion, as the New Testament is being written, there is still no record of the early church celebrating the birthday of Jesus. However, evergreens are still being used, and new converts to Christianity were still participating in Saturnalia celebrations; the Apostle Paul writes the following in 2 Corinthians chapter 6 which address this behavior: "(14) … for what fellowship have righteousness and iniquity? Or what fellowship has light with darkness? (15) What agreement has Christ with Belial? Or what portion has a believer with an unbeliever? (16) What agreement has a temple of God with idols? For you are a temple of the living God…" (2 Corinthians 6:14-16). Paul is encouraging them to take the direction Jesus laid out: live different, look different, and be a light to a world of darkness.

100 – 225 A.D.

One to two hundred years after Jesus' crucifixion, in the writings of early Christian writers such as Irenaeus (circa 130 – 200) and Tertullian (circa 160 – 225), there are still no records given of any celebrations of birth among Christians or the birth of Jesus. On the contrary, Origen of Alexandria (circa 165 – 264) mentions how Romans were celebrating their birth anniversaries, and in his writings he labels such celebrations as "pagan" practices.

200 A.D.

Much interest and curiosity now greatly increases to find the actual day of the Messiah's birth. Many scholars set out to pinpoint the day Christ was born with estimated guesses spanning from dates in late May to September. Even to this point in time, no one can agree on His actual birth date, and Christmas as a holiday surrounding the events of Jesus' birth is not being celebrated at all. Still, evergreens remain a strong part of winter solstice celebrations.

300 A.D.

In Rome, at the time Constantine (the first Christian Roman Emperor) came to power, it was 306 AD. Mithraism was the dominant religion, but Constantine slowly came to be converted to Christianity. Because of Constantine's conversion, Christianity became the religion of the state and public funds were utilized to build churches. Constantine soon commissioned the Church of the Nativity to be built in Bethlehem to honor where Christ was born. 336 A.D. was the first recorded date where Christmas was unofficially celebrated on December 25. This was in Rome under Emperor Constantine. Due to a four-fold combination of (a) growing public interest in Christ's day of birth, (b) the spreading of Christianity throughout Rome, (c) the Roman tradition of celebrating one's birth, and (d) the remaining strong influence of Saturnalia celebrations among most people, in the year 350 A.D. Pope Julius I would officially "assign" Jesus' birthday to December 25. This would eventually usher in the transfer of worship from the "sun" god to the Son of God. As the fifth century neared, other forms of Roman worship would soon be banned, and Christianity would begin spreading quickly.

As Christianity broadened among the peoples of pagan lands, numerous rituals of the Winter Solstice were melded with those of Christianity, because of the liberal governing of Pope Gregory I and the collaboration of the missionaries. That is, instead of teaching the converts to abandon their old superstitions and start a clean new life solely according to the word of God, the Church found it easier and more practical to give the old superstitions new names and mix Christianity with paganism. The use of the evergreen tree begins to blend in with Christian celebrations.

500 A.D.

In 529 A.D., Emperor Justinian declared Christmas a civic holiday. Jesus' name would eventually be associated with the tree by the Christian community, and the tree would slowly become known as the "Christmas tree."

700 A.D.

One popular Catholic legend of the Christmas tree origin shares a larger-than-life story of St. Boniface, known as the Apostle to the Germans. While on a mission trip in the region of Bavaria around 720 A.D., he came upon a barbaric annual ceremony. The townspeople intended to use a child as a human sacrifice around a giant oak tree named "Thunder Oak" for the worship of Thor. He boldly interrupted their ceremony, evangelized, and, challenging the power of Thor against the power of God, proceeded to chop down what they regarded as Thor's Tree. Then, while continuing to share the gospel of Jesus Christ, he pointed to a young fir tree nearby, saying,

> "This little tree, a young child of the forest, shall be your holy tree tonight. It is the wood of peace… It is the sign of an endless life, for its leaves are ever green. See how it points upward to heaven. Let this be called the tree of the Christ-child; gather about it, not in the wild wood, but in your own homes; there it will shelter no deeds of blood, but loving gifts and rites of kindness."

Chopping down the worship tree was exactly what Gideon did! However, despite good intentions, and contrary to Gideon's actions of obedience to God, St. Boniface replaced the ceremonial oak tree with the evergreen Christmas tree (oops!). Moved by the convicting actions and witnessing of St. Boniface that night, all the pagans were baptized and adopted the annual Christmas tree tradition in their homes.

1500 A.D.

Stories of a kind and benevolent bishop from the 3rd century (St. Nicholas) start to re-surface, and the legend of Father Christmas would evolve through the next four centuries, bringing us names such as Père Noël, St. Nick, Kris Kringle, Sinterklaas, and Santa Claus as the bringer of Christmas presents in stockings and under the tree.

1600 - 1700 A.D.

Early puritan settlers who came to America still feel Christmas activities were never of God, and therefore, stand firm to the belief that this holiday tradition is not appropriate. From 1659 to 1681 Christmas was outlawed in Boston where a fine of 5 shillings was issued to anyone exhibiting "Christmas spirit". The American Revolution influenced a decline in most English customs including Christmas celebrations.

1800 A.D.

In 1843, *A Christmas Carol* by Charles Dickens was published and its influence swept England and America into a new way of looking at Christmas. Because of Dicken's work, Christmas shifted from a raucous carnival event to a warm nostalgic focus on peace, family, benevolence and goodwill being spread toward mankind. This fresh perspective helped spark America's interest and justified the new acceptance of this old holiday. Americans adopted more of the "family focused" celebration traditions, sent greeting cards to family and close friends, lavished their kids with presents, and reached back about 100 years to revive some other traditions from the past. This festival was re-invented, picked up momentum, and the American government finally declared Christmas a federal holiday on June 26, 1870.

TODAY

Today, the Christmas tree tradition is just something most of us grew up participating in because our parents did. We as Christians hardly know anything about its true history, but we rely on stories we're told to perpetuate the tradition with intentions of honoring Christ. We hear the evergreen tree represents Christ's undying eternal life and love, the lights represent us being a light to the world, red and white candy canes signify Christ's purity and His blood shed for us, the angel or star atop the tree reminds us of Bethlehem, and the gifts under the tree represent God's gift to us… His son. Our joy-filled memories of past Christmas celebrations also seem to justify a continuation of those traditions. So, each year, we unpack the Christmas tree, decorate it, enjoy the lights and the presents underneath, and don't give it a second thought because that's what we've always done.

No matter what, most Christmas holiday and Christmas tree origin stories have one theme in common: the desire to worship other gods using evergreens in late December was slowly "replaced" over a span of hundreds of years with a desire to worship baby Jesus "Christ." This switch happened partly because of man's inability to separate from ingrained habits of winter solstice celebration traditions. Man's celebration focus slowly evolved from worshipping a "sun god" to worshipping the

"Son of God," but many of the tools and traditions remained.

Ultimately, over many centuries, the collective Christian community said non-verbally, "We can simply take a bad pagan holiday tradition we enjoy and turn it into something God-like, so that we can keep what we feel brings us joy. We can put Christ's name on it, put a star on the top to represent the star of Bethlehem, put presents underneath to signify selfless giving, consider the evergreen leaves as symbols of Christ's everlasting life and love, recognize the red and white stripes on candy canes as symbols of Jesus' blood and purity…" and on, and on, and on. They thought, "We can just take a not-so-good tradition of heathen god worship and *make* it good by putting our Holy God's name on it!" But friends, when you mix a little bad with good (or bad with God), it eventually destroys what is pure and the result never brings God's best for us (Galatians 5:9). A basic study of the four Gospels reveals that God never instituted any tree or any form of evergreen as a worship tool in honoring Himself, or the birth of Christ.

What we draw from a study of the history of Christmas and the Christmas tree is this: even though we don't bow down to the tree and worship it, or think of it as our "god" today, it was still used as a TOOL or symbol to worship other "gods" of heathen nations in the past.

PUZZLE PIECE #2:

To recap puzzle piece #2, the "tree" we now enjoy today in December, and the holiday we know as "Christmas"—because they were both used by other nations *first* to worship heathen gods and were never instituted by God—will always be *borrowed.* They are borrowed pagan TOOLS of worship upon which we have traded out the names of pagan gods and affixed the holy name of Christ.

- CHAPTER 8 -

BORROWING TRADITIONS

We've learned from Chapter 7 that history clearly shows both Christmas and the Christmas tree tradition were originally used as tools of pagan worship before we Christians took them, put Christ's name on them, and claimed them as our own. Nevertheless, because they came from somewhere else, no matter how many Christians or churches use them today, and no matter how many years we continue to use them, they will always be BORROWED.

SEEKING PUZZLE PIECE #3:

So, what's the big deal? Why can't we just borrow an old pagan tradition and use it in an honorable way toward God? Instead of asking ourselves that question, let's actually go to God and ask Him if He has any opinion about this idea. In fact, we can seek His guidance right now by turning in our Bibles to Deuteronomy 12, verses 29-32.

God answers this exact question in 1406 B.C., right before the Israelites cross over the Jordan to take the Promised Land. That's correct, 1400 years before His Son would ever be born, He answers the question about celebrating His Son's birth *and* His future birthdays that will follow! God's instructions in this matter are not only explicitly clear, but they also show just how deeply God opposes borrowed pagan tools of worship.

Starting in verse 29, God says "(29) When Yahweh your God cuts off the nations from before you, where you go in to dispossess them, and you dispossess them, and dwell in their land; (30) be careful that you are not ensnared to follow them, after that they are destroyed from before you; and that you not inquire after their gods, saying, 'How do these nations serve their gods? I will do likewise.' (31) You shall not do so to Yahweh your God"

In these three verses, God is telling His people, "Hey, when I destroy these nations before your very eyes, do not ask, 'Hmm… how did these nations serve their gods? I think I will worship my God in the same way.'"

He is saying, "Do not borrow or use the same pagan rituals to worship me, and since Jesus is Lord, that will include worship to the Son of God when He is born as well." This also includes ALL His assumed birthday parties forever! Here's how God feels about it:

In verse 31 we read, "… for every abomination to Yahweh, which He hates, have they done to their gods; for they even burn their sons and their daughters in the fire to their gods."

This passage is telling us that God *hates* every single tradition the pagans have used to worship their gods—every one! Do not be fooled into thinking that burning children is the *only* ritual that God has a problem with! Every pagan worship ritual—using trees, poles, or altars, and placing gifts at the base of these, sacrificing humans, engaging in orgies, drinking blood, using carved images in the likeness of animals He created, or worshipping through drunkenness or beastiality… He hates them *all*!

God's advice becomes very clear in verse 32 when He says, "Whatever thing I command you, that you shall observe to do. You shall not add to it, nor take away from it." Keep in mind that this phrase, "whatever I command you," applies to all commandments past, present, and future.

Deuteronomy 12:29-32 is only part 1 of a soft but firm lesson from Dad. I now invite you to picture a scene where a father is up on a hilltop with his child, just the two of them. He is about to impart to this child one of life's important lessons. In this imagined vision you now have, God is the father and we are the beloved child totally oblivious to the valuable life wisdom soon to be revealed from the father who abhors sin but eternally adores us!

Got that picture in your mind? Are you on the hilltop with Him?

Up until now, within this timeframe where God is on this proverbial hilltop speaking to Moses, Joshua, the Israelites, their future descendants, and yes eventually you and I through the book of Deuteronomy, God has taken his mighty finger of righteousness while we are standing beside Him on the hilltop and pointed the attention away from us for a softer teaching moment. While focusing our attention toward the evil nations, we hear Him say while He looks at them, "what you see over there…", pointing at the abomination itself, "don't do that!"

So for His part 2 finale of the impressionable teaching moment, He then turns to us, He squares up His shoulders with ours, looks us straight in the eye and imparts a commandment in our direction: Deuteronomy 16:21-22. With the same righteous finger now pointing at us, He says with a loving but firm voice, "You shall not plant for yourselves an Asherah of any kind of tree beside Yahweh your God's altar… I hate it!" Soft, but firm lesson. Soft, because we're standing at such a close face to face distance to Dad. Firm, because His voice resolutely echoes how much He abhors the abomination He just showed us on the hilltop. He wants to protect us from it.

Picture it how you wish, but this is how I create an image of God teaching me that trees added in any way to my worship to Him is not something He likes or wants.

When it comes to commandments of *how* to worship Him, we cannot add to or take away from them. We find in the Old Testament a vast array of incredibly specific instructions detailing how God was to be worshipped, both daily and annually. God listed in precise detail, in Exodus chapters 25-31 and Numbers chapters 2 through 10, specifications for building the ark of the covenant, how many rings to put on the curtains (along with their colors and lengths) in the holy of holies, the exact recipe for the fragrant incense used in worship, precisely who could become priests and how they should enter the tent, and the exact layout of the Jewish lunar celebration feasts calendar, sixteen chapters of explicit detail!

In the New Testament, we see examples of how to live, how to love each other, how to pray, how to worship God in spirit and in truth, how to treat our neighbors and our enemies, and how, when, and why to take the Lord's Supper. In both covenants, God was clear we should not add to or take away from the commandments of how to worship Him.

When we worship God in a way He has specifically told us to avoid at all cost, it does not matter how sincere our heart is; God is displeased. Remember when Aaron's sons went into the tent burning incense the wrong way? "Nadab and Abihu, the sons of Aaron, each took his censer, and put fire in it, and laid incense on it, and offered strange fire before Yahweh, which He had not commanded them. (2) Fire came out from before Yahweh, and devoured them, and they died before Yahweh." (Leviticus 10:1-2) All they did was slightly alter the incense and God killed them! We could ask ourselves: are we *adding* to the commandments of worship when we add or modify pagan traditions to worship Him and call them Christmas?

READING ASSIGNMENT

Read Exodus chapters 25-31 and marvel at how detailed our God is when it comes to describing exactly how He wanted to be worshipped by His people in the Old Testament.

If God wanted us to use Christmas as a way to celebrate the birth of His son, how magnificently precise do you think His description would have been? Yet, with all of the hyper-accurate details God revealed in both Old and New Testaments, not once did He ever describe, show desire or preference for, command, or authorize the use of an erected tree as a form, tool, or symbol to be used in worship or to honor Him. Neither did He give us a date or even a single word of instruction to focus on Jesus' birth. However, in stark contrast, God did give an exact date and precise time of Jesus' death. He also gave a command to celebrate it through communion (Lord's Supper) while looking forward to His return (1 Cor. 11:23-26).

We have spent so much time and energy throughout numerous generations trying to perfect the way we celebrate the birth of Christ during the Christmas holidays, but all this has been according to our own understanding. Did anyone ever stop and ask God, "LORD, how do you want to be honored during this time?" If we will just lean on God, He promises to make our paths straight. (Proverbs 3:5-6)

So, what do we draw from all of this? In the book of Deuteronomy, God forbids the use of borrowed pagan rituals, borrowed pagan traditions, and borrowed pagan worship tools to honor or worship Him. He also forbids a tree of any form to be associated with worship to Him.

PUZZLE PIECE #3:

Therefore, our third piece of the puzzle is: God HATES traditions that are BORROWED and recycled to worship Him! Even with our best intentions, sweetest sincerity, or finest decorations, they are still an abomination to Him!

- CHAPTER 9 -

BIRTHDAY PARTY FOR JESUS?

We're now going to focus on the last of our jigsaw pieces as we uncover the secrets of the history of Christ's birthday celebrations!

SEEKING PUZZLE PIECE #4:

Do you remember the second "God-centered" question from earlier that was asked: Did God institute a holiday to worship the birth of His son Jesus? I want you to really think about Jesus' birth for a moment. The only time the Bible celebrates His birthday was the very day of His birth. There was baby Jesus, Mary and Joseph, animals, shepherds, angels praising God and making announcements… they had quite a party! Yes, I know the wise men came to give gifts, but that was two years later. They were just fashionably late to the first party!

The book of Luke contains the famous birth announcement from an angel to the shepherds… "For there is born to you today, in David's city, a Savior, who is Christ the Lord" (Luke 2:11). Now, who did God say this was? It wasn't "Little Joe" or even "Joseph Jr."… it was Christ! Even in baby form, He was named our LORD and our SAVIOR, as the one we need to be lifting up, exalting, and worshipping for who He has always been (Lord) and what He would soon become (Savior)!.

Read it one more time: "For there is born to you this day in the city of David"… who? A baby in swaddling clothes? No! It was a savior! And how does one become a savior? By living a completely sin-free life according to the Old Law, following the heavenly Father's will above your own—even to the point of being beaten beyond recognition, driven to Golgotha, hung on a cross, forsaken by God almighty—all because of a deep love for sinners who couldn't pay their own penalty.

But wait! Baby Jesus had not done all these things *yet*! My friends, this announcement was not a baby announcement; it was a thirty-three-year-in-advance prophecy of a life-giving Savior that, praise God, would later purchase eternal salvation for all mankind. The future was being celebrated! But what about prophecies of a virgin birth, you ask? And what about prophecies of a baby being born in Bethlehem? All the prophesies in the Old Testament mentioning a coming baby were never intended to make us fixate on the birth of an infant. Rather, by declaring Him as Immanuel, Messiah, an everlasting ruler, and our Savior, these prophesies established solid validation and genuinely authenticated the identity of the one who would claim to be the Son of God, and also gave credence to Jesus' life, His purpose, and ultimately the power of His coming death and resurrection!

Notice that God does not give us a specific day to return to for future birthday parties. No parties were thrown by the apostles as examples for us to follow in the gospels. No parties were enjoyed or recorded by the early Christians in the book of Acts. And no birthday date was ever mentioned by Luke, Paul, or John throughout the entire New Testament! Why do you think this is the case?

To answer that question, let's change direction for a moment. I want you to notice that Jesus' death on the cross did happen at a very, very specific time! It was the day after He shared a Passover meal with His apostles: Friday, April 3, A.D. 33 at the "Ninth Hour," or three p.m.

You may ask, "How can we possibly know the exact date and time so specifically? There's no Bible verse that gives us such incredible detail!" And you're right; there is no single verse. But by piecing together seven great clues that God embedded into the scriptures, we find He wants us to know the exact moment when it happened.

For just a minute, we're going to take a small tangent I think you'll enjoy. There was a man by the name of Jimmy Akin who did a fantastic study sharing seven clues in the Bible that precisely pinpoint the crucifixion of Jesus. I encourage you to look up his presentation, but here are the highlights:

- ✞ CLUE #1 – We know Jesus was crucified during the high priesthood of Caiaphas (high priest from A.D. 18-37). This is found in Matthew 26:57 and John 11:49-51.

- ✞ CLUE #2 – Matthew 27:11-13, Mark 15:1-15, Luke 23:1-24, and John 19:1-16 tell us this happened during the governorship of Pontius Pilate (Governor A.D. 26-36). Now, with these two clues alone, we have a ten-year window of possible dates between A.D. 26 and A.D. 36.

- ✞ As we continue, CLUE #3 comes from Luke 3:1 and tells us that Jesus' ministry did not start until after John the Baptist began his ministry in 29 A.D., coinciding with the fifteenth year of Tiberius Caesar… thus further narrowing the ten-year window.

- ✞ CLUE #4 marks His death on a Friday (aka Preparation Day), one day before Sabbath, found in Matthew 27:62, Mark 15:42, Luke 23:54, and John 19:31 and 42.

- ✞ CLUE #5 further narrows our search to a Friday during Passover celebration (not just any Passover). This comes from Matthew 26:1-2 and 17, Mark 14:1, Luke 22:7-13, and John 18:39. A careful look at the Jewish feasts calendar shows only two possible Passover preparation Fridays within this date range: either Friday, April 7 A.D. 30 or Friday, April 3 A.D. 33.

- ✞ To distinguish between the Passover Friday of A.D. 30 or A.D. 33, we look to the book of John for CLUE #6 and find in John 2:13, John 6:4, and John 11:55 that Jesus and His Apostles participated in three separate Passover celebrations before the Passover of His death.

- ✞ Since Jesus' three-year ministry began after John the Baptist's ministry began in A.D. 29, then this eliminates A.D. 30, leaving us with only one possible day. But isn't our God amazing? He goes one step further in Matthew 27:45-50, Mark 15:33-37, and Luke 23:44-46 to give us CLUE #7. He marks the exact time of Jesus giving up His spirit at the ninth hour, or what we know as three p.m.

- ✞ And so, in an event worthy of infinite universal celebration, our Lord Jesus delivered the massive blow to Satan by giving up His perfect spirit on Friday, April 3, A.D. 33 at three p.m.

Hold your thoughts on the precise pinpoint of His death; we will come back to that.

We are commanded to celebrate Jesus' death and resurrection each time we partake in the Lord's Supper. Between His birth and death, Jesus' death, burial, and resurrection were significantly more powerful, resulting in the releasing of bondage of all sin for all people for all time, giving everyone direct access to the Father and securing a place in heaven for everyone for all eternity! It's almost as if God designed it so that we would *not* get hyper-focused on a day of birth, but instead would find value and celebration in His death and resurrection!

Remember in Matthew 17:1-5 when Peter was on the mount for the transfiguration? When Peter saw Jesus, Moses, and Elijah, he immediately jumped the gun with a sincere desire to show honor by suggesting to build three shelters (or tabernacles)—one to honor each of them. Despite Peter's sincerity to show honor, God intervened and stopped that idea in its tracks. Had Peter been successful in his well-intended, sincere, but ignorant idea, he would have unintentionally put Jesus in a proverbial box and elevated Moses and Elijah to a status equal to Jesus Christ. What a mess that would have made!

Sadly, in the same manner as Peter, when we rushed in with good intentions to assign a birthday to Jesus without consulting God's direction or instruction, we detrimentally put Jesus in a box, assigning Him with 364 "Non-Birthdays." Even if that doesn't sound so bad, it means we have now elevated Santa and other holiday traditions to a level they don't belong, and we seem to have been tricked by Satan to focus on a helpless baby, not a liberating savior!

PUZZLE PIECE #4:

As we wrap up PUZZLE PIECE #4, here is what we can draw from these scriptures:

- There is no God-given birth date for Jesus
- God gives no official mandate to celebrate His Son's birth (so even if a date had been given, there were no instructions detailing *how* to celebrate it)
- There are no documented birthday parties for Jesus to serve as examples for us to follow
- There is an absolute specific time of death, burial, and resurrection
- There is a mandate to celebrate the death, burial, and resurrection
- There are specific instructions on *how* to celebrate His death through the Lord's Supper

Remember when I said hold on to that thought about pinpointing an exact time of crucifixion? We cannot always lazily look for a single verse to answer precise questions and then give up if it's not gift-wrapped for us in one tight scripture. In the same manner, we can't just give up if God does not lay out one easy verse on how to worship Him during the holidays! Through diligence of searching, we now have four solid puzzle pieces that can be assembled to reveal a solid truth, and our God promises He is a rewarder of those who diligently seek Him. I hope you'll stay with me for the next chapter, where we reveal a reward for our diligence in seeking out an answer to the question:

Lord, how do YOU want to be worshipped during the Christmas holidays?

- CHAPTER 10 -

PUZZLE PIECE RECAP

In Hebrews 11:6, we read, "Without faith it is impossible to be well pleasing to Him, for he who comes to God must believe that He exists, and that He is a rewarder of those who seek Him with diligence." This verse promises that diligence in seeking God (or His will) guarantees a reward. Sometimes we may think of a reward as something that brings us pleasure, but if we think in terms of a treasure hunt, a reward could actually be the revealing clue of which direction to turn next, or a warning to protect you from approaching danger, which makes the treasure hunt safer and much more productive. The treasure of our hunt is to be closer to God by understanding what He wants more clearly. We just uncovered four important puzzle pieces, which can help guide us to that treasure we are seeking. Our reward comes right after this recap:

Four Puzzle Pieces:

1. Idols are useless tools of worship to other gods, and the use of them is forbidden by our God. God wants NO part of idols; no part in any way (Jeremiah 10).

2. The Christmas tree is indeed a form of, or a "tool" of, pagan worship from the past. We borrowed it and put our Savior's name on it—even if it was with good intentions. Nevertheless, it was still PAGAN, and it is still BORROWED.

3. God says not to ever take pagan worship rituals/traditions and BORROW them, put His holy name on them, then use them to worship Him; He hates this (Deuteronomy 12).

4. God gives no official mandate nor examples anywhere in scripture to celebrate Christ's birthday, but He brilliantly reveals His death with stunning and magnificent detail (Matthew, Mark, Luke, John).

Now let's take these four pieces and connect them together. Our message sounds like this:

GOD wants no part of idols, including the Christmas tree, which was a pagan tool we borrowed. GOD hates it when we use a borrowed Christmas celebration and a borrowed tree to worship Him. He emphasized His Son's death much more than He highlighted Jesus' birth. If we focus more on His Son's death and resurrection, we will find He has given us our WORTH, FREEDOM, IDENTITY, AUTHORITY, and POWER!

It is through the DEATH and resurrection of Lord Jesus that we discover our worth is established in John 3:16; our freedom is proclaimed in Romans 8:1-3; our identity is proven from 2 Corinthians 5:21; our authority is affirmed from Luke 10:19; and our power is assured by Romans 8:11!

I'm sure you're familiar with the phrase, "he can't see the forest for the trees." Well, I am suggesting that, because of certain Christmas traditions we have naturally been born into and followed, we are not seeing God and Christ as clearly as He desires to be seen. We let other things top our Christmastime top ten list; we let some (not all) traditions push God out of the spotlight. We take honor and glory only reserved for God Himself and give it away to fictitious characters. We let the world and traditions tell us how we should be relating to God rather than asking God how He wants to be seen, honored, worshipped, and glorified.

In short, I am saying that when we all unpack the noble firs, the green giants, and the blue spruces from the attic, dress them up, and follow the leader through the reindeer games of holiday "tradition," we all have a hard time seeing God… through the trees. For most people, that can be really hard to hear, and I understand, because I was there too. It's tempting and much easier to just suppress the truth and continue enjoying the traditions that have brought us so many happy memories. It's much simpler to avoid change and enjoy what we know.

Gideon was in the same predicament when God showed up and revealed the truth to him. But we all need to beware of suppressing the truth, as Romans 1:18 says, "For the wrath of God is revealed from heaven against all ungodliness and unrighteousness of men who suppress the truth…" It can be very scary to get to a point in your life where you say, "I know what God said and I know what I should do; I just don't want to do that… and I don't want to talk about it."

I want to take this time and make a huge disclaimer here. God never told us that we couldn't worship Him on December 25. In fact, we can worship Jesus any day of the year, and I know God would love for us to worship Him every day of the year. We just don't need a tree to do that! In fact, God loves us, and God loves our worship to Him, but what we are learning is that God doesn't want the tree to come between Him and us.

What I have just unfolded for you is that God is taking issue with *how* He wants to be worshipped (or how He *doesn't* want to be worshipped). Our study will take a little bit of a split direction as we move forward, but the simple version of what we will soon discover is that we need go to God's word constantly (not just for Christmas activities) and we always need to ask the Holy Spirit to reveal truth to us where God's word speaks or does not speak on any particular issue. One solid fact we can take confidence in is The Holy Spirit will never contradict God's word and will never lead us in the wrong direction.

Friends, I want you to take heart and be encouraged as we move on, because if you choose a path like Gideon and renounce, or even reconsider, a particular tradition in your life based on the prompting of the Holy Spirit in an attempt to honor God, I promise you, God will be just as faithful to lift you up as He was to Gideon!

God is no respecter of persons, but He is a respecter of obedience… especially in the face of persecution.

For me and my household, reading only Jeremiah and Deuteronomy and researching the origin of the "Christmas tree" is enough to make it obvious that participating in activities with the Christmas tree is not how God desires to be worshipped, nor will it bring God's absolute best blessings for my family. Keep in mind, the tree doesn't automatically block God's goodness or faithfulness to you. We've had a Christmas tree in the past, and God has most assuredly blessed our family hundreds, if not thousands, of times, but in our spiritual walk we finally came to a crossroads of truth versus tradition with Christmas, and we chose to let Gideon be our role model. We took the path described by Robert Frost (the road less traveled). I believe the "choice" we made in our heart to put God and Jesus over the Christmas tree is what opened the floodgates of more blessings that followed.

By way of reading this book, you are now coming to the crossroads of truth versus tradition. Whether experiencing a visitation by an angel or by receiving a word from God through this book (either way, it's exactly like God showing up in person to reveal truth to you), right now, He is revealing His preference of being honored, even in the holiday season, and He's revealing it to YOU. Now, the best thing you can do is to follow His voice, follow the truth, no matter what persecution lies ahead. In the end, I guarantee you will get closer to God, and He can do amazing miracles FOR you and THROUGH you, just like He did with Gideon!

I'm not out to steal future happy holiday moments by suggesting the removal of your Christmas tree. Instead, I want to invite you and escort you to a place where even happier moments overflow, by encouraging you to live with a character of obedience and honor to God and His instructions, just like Gideon! I desire amazing miracles for my family, and I want amazing miracles to be done for others through my family. I also wish for God to shower more blessings on you and your family! So here I am, sharing the truth of God's word and bringing you to your moment in the crossroads.

At this point in our discussion, God has firmly established His position through His word, yet a small few may still argue that these are Old Testament scriptures, which don't apply to us today. To this, I encourage you to read these Old and New Testament scriptures: Malachi 3:6; Numbers 23:19; Isaiah 46:9-11; Ezekiel 24:14; Hebrews 13:8; and James 1:17. God is the same yesterday, today, and forever, especially when it comes to the things He says He hates or despises, or are an abomination to Him.

I promise you, God is not saying, "Do you remember that whole business a long time ago about not using borrowed pagan traditions to worship me? Well, there are so many good people doing it now and I don't see anyone sacrificing children anymore, so I guess times have changed… it is the 21st century after all." Friends, if any of you think God's position on things that are holy versus unholy has changed, please reread the passages above! God's opinion has not and will not change… ever! This includes His position on unholy rituals.

There is a place for God. There is a place for Jesus Christ. There is a place for Christmas holiday traditions. There is a place for the Christmas tree. There is a place for the word of God. As we move into the next chapter, we finally get to assemble a lot of information we've learned and put all of these in their proper places.

- CHAPTER 11 -

EVERYTHING HAS A PLACE

Everything has a place. Where does the Christmas tree belong in our worship of Jesus? God, knowing that one day His people would redirect pagan worship practices toward Him, warned us in 1406 B.C. not to go in this direction. The Christmas tree never had a place in our worship to God and never will. I believe the Bible is very clear on that one. It doesn't belong.

Where do other Christmas traditions belong in our worship of Jesus? Specifically, how should we treat traditions like displaying manger scenes, attending candlelight masses, giving gifts, drinking hot chocolate, taking sleigh rides, spending time with the family, making snowmen, having snowball fights, singing or caroling, reading the book of Luke's account of Christ's birth? You're going to have to let the Holy Spirit lead you on all these things. I am confident the Holy Spirit will never lead you in the wrong direction. If you seek the Spirit's guidance and cross-check it with God's word, following where both are leading, you can never go wrong.

So, where does *Christ* belong in Christmas? Jesus was brought into this world to testify to truth… and to save our souls. Jesus and His word, which are one and the same (John 1:1-14), both belong in our hearts and on our minds every day, all day (Joshua 1:8), and above all holidays. Seasons change. Jesus does not. When we pull Jesus into a holiday period that begins right after Thanksgiving and ends just before the New Year and say things like, "Jesus is the reason for the season," there is a soft subliminal message that follows: "When the season is over, we can pack up Jesus, put Him in the Christmas box, and say, "See you at Easter!"

Considering the way many lives and behaviors are currently influenced during this time of year, my wife Rachelle regretfully yet perceptively remarks, "The Christmas Season is the reason we need Jesus!"

To finalize, Jesus is so much more than the reason for one winter holiday. Jesus is the reason for all four seasons, all twelve months, each and every one of the 365.242199 days of the year (I went ahead and threw in the decimals out of respect for calculated leap years). He is the reason for all we do. Jesus is the reason for who we are, why we exist. Jesus is the reason we have promises of the

Kingdom of Heaven that are being fulfilled, and for everything that lies ahead for all mankind. He is the reason we can spend eternity with a God who loves us more than our mortal minds could ever know. He is not just a silly season!

Jesus deserves center stage for all our praise and honor for what He has done for us, and for how much He loves us. Jesus has NO PLACE where He is forced to share the spotlight with Santa Claus or "Father Christmas," Rudolph, Christmas parades, or anything else we think Christmas might be, and we dishonor Him with a tree tradition that His father clearly despises and never instituted. If we really want to honor Christ, then every word needs to honor Him, as does every thought, every day of the year. Don't wait until Christmas to give Him extra honor, praise, and acknowledgement! And don't put Santa on God's throne!

Wait, we haven't put Santa in God's position… have we?

- CHAPTER 12 -

DOES GOD GIVE SANTA MILK & COOKIES?

Does Santa Claus bring honor to God? If God's word tells us not to lie (Leviticus 19:11; Proverbs 12:22; Proverbs 13:5; Proverbs 14:5; John 8:44; Colossians 3:9), then what are we doing trying to convince our children that the blessings they receive on Christmas day come from a jolly red elf who lives at the North Pole and rides in a magic sleigh pulled by flying reindeer (one of which has a glowing red nose), who knows when they're sleeping and when they're awake, who sees all their deeds, good or bad, and who delivers the good things they ask him for? If you say, "But Santa is not a lie; he is the spirit of goodness in all of us as we give to our children," you need to hold on and wait for more than just a "New York minute."

Be very careful; if you believe the statement that Santa is the spirit of goodness in us, then you just replaced the Holy Spirit with a fictitious fat elf! The Spirit of God lives in us (1 Corinthians 3:16; 1 Corinthians 6:19; 2 Corinthians 6:16; 2 Timothy 1:14; Romans 8:11; John 16:13; Romans 8:9; Galatians 4:6; 1 John 2:27), and all good things come from God (James 1:17). There are qualities reserved for God and God alone. When we support the stories of Santa, we rob God of the honor only He deserves. The lies of Santa dishonor God and can potentially set children up for a fall from faith.

If you think I'm exaggerating, look at the table on the next page and compare some of our most common Christmas lies with the corresponding Christian truths that we should be reinforcing in their precious, impressionable, and most valuable minds:

What we tell our children about SANTA:	Bible reference:	What we should be teaching our children about GOD:
Santa is jolly (filled with joy).	1 John 4:8; Nehemiah 8:10	God is the only being filled completely with love, and His Joy is our strength!
Santa knows when you are sleeping, when you're awake, when you're bad or good.	Matthew 6:8; Luke 12:7; Psalm 33:13-15; Jeremiah 23:23-24; Proverbs 15:3; Hebrews 4:13	God knows what you need before you ask; He sees all good and all bad, He even knows the number of hairs on your head! Even with our deepest secrets, nothing is hidden from Him… NOTHING!
Santa lives in a place we can't see or visit (Workshop at the North Pole).	Jeremiah 23:23-24; 1 Kings 8:43; Matthew 6:9; Hebrews 9:24 1 Corinthians 3:16; 1 Kings 8:27; Ephesians 2:22	In Jeremiah, God tells us He fills both heaven and earth. The New Testament tells us God lives inside us. As a spirit being, God is everywhere.
Santa delivers what we ask for and gives good gifts.	John 15:7; Luke 12:32; Psalms 35:27	God wants to bless all His children. It is His good pleasure and delight to bless us.
Santa can do magical & impossible things.	Matthew 19:26	With God all things are possible!
Santa visits those who believe in him.	Romans 1:17; Galatians 3:11; Hebrews 10:38	Without faith, it is impossible to please God, and the Righteous shall live by faith… in God.

We have just considered several characteristics that are reserved for God and God alone. When we superimpose these qualities onto Santa, it is a form of stealing honor from God and having our Lord "share" the throne with Santa. It is a subtle form of dethroning our God. Satan (the Devil) wanted to do the same thing from the beginning, and God threw him out of the heavenly kingdom along with one-third of all the angels who went along with his scheme to dethrone God (Ezekiel 28:11-19; Revelation 12). But placing Santa on God's throne is not the only subliminal, destructive thing we are doing to our children. These Santa stories we weave into our children's impressionable minds work to slowly dissolve the solid pillars of truth, which they need to rely on in order to stand firm in their faith when a rough day of spiritual warfare comes to attack their belief in God.

Watch how this little example illustrates the way parents could potentially harm the critical decision-making moment of an older teenager being released into the world to be on their own: We tell our young children, "Trust us (adults), there is someone out there you can't see, who is full of joy and cares about everyone, including you and your happiness. We sing songs about him. He knows everything! When you're awake, he knows. When you're asleep, he knows! When you do good, he knows. When you do bad, he knows! Send him your requests by means of letters mailed to a place you can't visit to tangibly verify his existence. Forget about verification, just believe with faith! He lives in a magical kingdom with lots of helpers to deliver what is most desirable in your heart. So, you better watch out, you better be good for the sake of goodness—He's coming… he's coming soon… he's coming to town."

When those impressionable minds reach a certain age, we reveal the "truth" that this mythical old man is NOT REAL! He is just created to bring hope and happiness into a troubled world. We say, "I know I told you to trust me THEN, but you can trust me today. Now that you're old enough and smart enough to handle the truth, here it is: he doesn't know everything, he doesn't answer your letters, he doesn't have a magical kingdom with lots of helpers, and there's really no need to be good for Santa Claus's sake. He's not coming to town because he DOES NOT REALLY EXIST."

Once we get all that straightened out in their minds, we pile the kids in the car on Sunday and drive to church to worship and sing songs about a joy-filled miracle being that lives in a place we cannot see. We tell the kids, "trust me!" He knows your heart, He knows when you sin, and He knows when you bless others. We try to convince them that He loves us and has our best interest at heart. We can send Him our requests through prayer, and He hears and answers those prayers. He lives in a place we cannot visit, with winged beings that He created as helpers. Even though we can't see Him or where He resides, we believe all this by faith. And once you're saved, you need to be good for His sake because one day He's coming… He's coming soon… He's coming back for us.

If you convincingly support the LIE of Santa, then what makes you so trustworthy when it comes to the TRUTH of God? Some might argue you can't blame the lie of Santa if children fall away from the faith. Although the lie itself can at least explain a small part of the influence, the real focus is not on the lie itself, but on the character and trustworthiness of the one telling the lie! If Santa Claus is not real, then what is he?

This is a great opportunity to segue into a fantastic description of what Santa Claus really is. While researching for this book, I came across a fabulous presentation about the three "D's" that represent Santa. I got this information from Todd Friel, the host of wretched.org, and I want to share it with you now. Santa is *Deception, Distraction*, and *Distortion.* I've added some of my own thoughts to Todd's presentation, but here's the breakdown:

1. SANTA IS DECEPTION (DISHONESTY)

In short, you're being dishonest. Dear friends, listen carefully. When you lie, you are a liar. The flames of a lying tongue can so quickly burn the bridges of trust. Trustworthiness, after telling a lie, is so hard to regain. It is difficult for anyone, especially a child, to have faith in a liar. Yes, we want our children to trust us, but even more importantly, we want our character of truthfulness to represent the God who made us and who we worship.

Follow me, if you will, through this irony: I'm created by a good God who tells me not to lie and commands me to tell the world (and my children) about Him and His great goodness. He also commands me to stand apart from, and be a light to, a world that wants me to compromise my faith and my values, look like them, act like them, and say, "no harm done, let's just have fun." I am His ambassador of truth. However, when I follow the crowd and I tell one of their harmless "white lies" to my children, I dishonor and degrade the perfect God of truth. Then I hypocritically turn to teach my children how important it is to get to know God and His goodness that calls me to demonstrate His good character (the very same good character that should keep me from telling lies). Is this what my God wants? Really?

Sharing the lie of Santa Claus brings dishonor to the God who made us. It desecrates the character of goodness that He desires to transform us into and destroys the trustworthiness we should have as His ambassadors to the world. The spreading of the lie of Santa weakens the believability in a God who is always faithful and trustworthy! Santa does not bring honor to God. Satan (the devil) does not bring honor to God either. He wants us to be just like him… liars!

2. SANTA IS DISTRACTION

Jesus should be the entire focus in any celebration dedicated to Him. Imagine if you were at a party to celebrate your birthday and everyone spent the majority of the time focusing on, singing to, talking to, sitting beside, talking about, laughing with, and honoring some other guy they brought to the party whom you don't even know! Not only would it make you feel insignificant, but the most important issue would be the lack of honor or respect from the people who set out to lift you up with recognition in the first place. If anyone deserves all honor, glory, and respect at a party for Jesus, it's not Santa—it's Jesus!

Any amount of time we spend on other things like Santa Claus, giving presents out of compulsion or presents with Santa's name on them, reading *'Twas the Night Before Christmas*, or any other Santa traditions that are replacing the character of God is time NOT being spent on Jesus. Santa is a distraction that takes time and focus away from our quest to put Jesus first in every part of our lives (whether in December or any other month).

3. SANTA IS DISTORTION

Some people use Santa to establish "common ground" in conversations with intentions of witnessing about God by paralleling the similar characteristics of both.

There is nothing wrong with a desire to share the gospel or lead people to God, Jesus, or salvation, but using Santa as a bridge can do more harm than good. To explain, allow me to unveil Satan's game plan:

Consider Ephesians 6:12, "For our wrestling [*battle*] is not against flesh and blood [*each other*], but against the principalities, … powers, … rulers of the darkness of this age, and against the spiritual forces of wickedness in the heavenly places [*invisible spiritual realm*]." Satan is the leader of these invisible principalities, and his weapons against us are lies and deception to keep us from knowing absolute truth. Our invisible battle as Christians is against ANYTHING that threatens to distort God's pure truth. Only the perfect truth of who God really is, and the undiluted truth of who we are in Christ can properly influence the decisions we make and actions we take enough to bring the greatest honor and glory to God (i.e. If Satan can simply distort the truth of who God really is, then God receives less glory from our misguided actions).

Stories and legends of Santa did not come from God. Satan, using whispers on shoulders, with all the time in the world from the third century until today, set out to create a character we Christians would embrace like a Trojan Horse! This imaginary personality of joy and benevolence had to be larger than life in each aspect, but short of God in every one. Satan began weaving the tale, and he gave us just what he wanted us to want. And so today, after swallowing hook, line, sinker… and saddle, some Christians not only embrace this Trojan Sleigh driver, but they use him in evangelizing, mistakingly drawing a holey analogy to a Holy God. End result: God's true nature is diluted, distorted, and misunderstood. Satan wins that match!

Now that you know the game plan from the "Father of Lies," let's compare and contrast the qualities of God and Jesus (who are one and the same & interchangeable) versus Santa observing the delicate differences between the two. Examine with me how the weapon of subtle distortion from this roaring lion (who seeks to devour us) allows Satan to easily leave "Claus marks" in his victims.

The reason we behave well for Santa is because he requires it BEFORE the gift is given. ("He knows if you've been bad or good, so be good for goodness sake!" Or, if you're bad, you get a lump of coal for Christmas.) With Santa, we must earn our gift!

The reason we behave well for Jesus is because we are responding to a gift that has already been given to us. Jesus has already given His gift, and we honor His request to love others out of thankfulness after the fact. "But God commends His own love toward us, in that while we were yet sinners, Christ died for us" (Romans 5:8). With Jesus, our eternal gift is His unearned, unmerited favor! Santa only gives gifts. God and Jesus not only give us gifts, but also wisdom, value, identity, power, authority, favor, and salvation (I'm sure there's even more somewhere).

On the surface, it may seem like an insignificant difference, but "being good" in the Santa example requires constant action on man's part to keep on earning. When paralleling the nature of Santa to the nature of God, people can get confused, assuming they too must "earn" their salvation, just like earning Santa's present. But believing in Jesus is simply renewing your mind's understanding that salvation already came from God, and our physical surrendering of trying to earn salvation is the only way to access salvation.

Since these two ways of receiving the gift are diametrically opposed, it is impossible to use Santa to draw a parallel to God. Even a small distortion can make a huge difference when salvation is on the line! Santa is distortion.

It is not my intention to steal away future happy holiday moments by removing Santa Claus, but I do want to help you open the door to even happier moments God will bring to those who choose not to blend in, but to stand out by living in the character of honesty to your children. When Christians blend in, it is IMPOSSIBLE to stand out.

God doesn't want us to follow the crowd! He wants us to be set apart for His name, be a city set on a hill, be a light to a dark world (Matthew 5:14-16). He wants us to be transformed into His likeness (Romans 8:29; 12:2; 2

Corinthians 3:18). When Christians stand out, it is IMPOSSIBLE to blend in.

Which do you choose? Jesus told us He only does what the father shows Him to do. (John 5:19). Jesus teaches us to follow God's lead.

God does not set out a plate of cookies on Christmas Eve… so why should we?

- CHAPTER 13 -

WORLDLY ARGUMENTS vs. BIBLICAL DEFENSES

As I shared with you earlier, it is our job as Christians to look different with the purpose of leading the world to change. As our lives hopefully provoke questions from the world, we must be prepared with explanations for why our faith calls us to live differently. Sharing the truth in love and being ready with a soft but convicted answer can be powerful enough to make an eternal difference in someone else's life. We must be prepared!

We've already seen from Deuteronomy why some traditions are not the best for Christians to participate in, but it may be hard to understand for some who have not read through this book or have not been introduced to the same scriptures we studied. It is our purpose to help them break the ties and separate from traditions we are confident and convinced God doesn't like. They may question why

Christmas could ever be considered wrong in God's eyes. They may even present arguments for why Christmas, the tree, and Santa Claus are Biblical necessities for sharing the gospel or they might try to explain why these items of tradition are so important for us to "save" in order to worship God.

But, because of what God has revealed to us throughout our Bible study so far, we are now well equipped with knowledge and wisdom to face and address any questions, arguments, or excuses people may present in trying to keep, save, or hang on to a tradition they may personally feel too attached to let go. This is not a time to argue. Don't face off against these Christian brothers and sisters. Instead, be kind. Be soft. Be gentle. Be loving, understanding, and empathetic. And through this kindly approach, you can slowly introduce the knowledge and the wisdom that helped you learn the truth. Most importantly, it's not your job to change a heart. Share with compassion, then turn them loose and let the Holy Spirit guide them to a conviction.

At the beginning of this book, there was a set of starter questions that focused on what "we" think and what "we" feel about the Christmas issues. Then I shared three "God-centered" questions and told you that once you put God's desires first in working through and answering those three questions, the answers to all other questions about Christmas will easily fall into place. This works because it doesn't matter what *we* think; it only matters what God thinks! We're about to experience that right here.

In order to prepare you to be "... ready to give an answer to everyone who asks you..." (1 Peter 3:15), I have assembled a few well-known worldly arguments you may come across and have also included informative Bible-based rebuttals for each one. In each example we will begin briefly with what the worldly (or carnal) position of the argument is, and then we will use our knowledge from the scriptures we studied to prepare you to politely refute any position that does not line up with the word of God.

COMMON WORLDLY ARGUMENTS

1. THERE IS A "WAR ON CHRISTMAS"

Worldly Argument:

It has been suggested that there is a "war on Christmas." People who want to "save" Christmas have cynically labeled those of us seeking to follow God's word (rather than tradition) with names like "Pagan scrooges" and "religious nitpickers." The former group paints a picture that we who want to know and follow God's instructions are party-pooping killjoys who only want to point fingers of condemnation, throw a wet blanket over

Christmas activities, and steal away all the fun from everybody.

Rebuttal:

This is not the case. First of all, there is no war against each other (Ephesians 6:12), only against forces of wickedness in the spiritual realm. This situation is exactly the same as a preacher at church who might teach a lesson about the need to forgive and restore with the same character and nature of God. Forgiving freely and endlessly (seventy times seven), praying for those who spitefully hurt you, blessing those who curse you, and exhibiting mercy to the undeserving with intention of restoration. Because some church members may be struggling in this stage of their own spiritual development, this hard message (and spiritual growth challenge) may be uncomfortable to hear and difficult to apply. There is no war in any of these sermon topics; there is only God's truth being illuminated by a preacher who is challenging self-reliant church members to be transformed into the likeness of, and the dependence on, God. Shining the light of truth brings conviction to those in the shadows, which provides an opportunity for change from a willing heart. It would be ridiculous for the members comfortable in their dark corners to jump up and cry out, "You're starting a war on our rights to harbor bitterness and unforgiveness, withhold mercy, be defensive, and protect ourselves from a cutting and hurtful world!" No, out of love, the preacher just explains that God's beautiful and more valuable gift of restoration sometimes arrives through the unpleasant corridors of our willingness to forgive. Sometimes the *one* message we don't want to listen to is the *only* message that provides the needed rescue. God, our holy general in the spirit realm, has given the command to forgive and forget as He does, and He knows if we choose to break free from that formidable stronghold of bitterness, unforgiveness, and lies of self-preservation embedded in our minds… and charge forward in the spiritual battle with the weapons of compassion and pardon, then the end of our personal journey through that scary corridor of forgiving our perpetrators surprisingly rises us up out of our own ashes and reveals a glorious restoration for BOTH undeserving parties unto Him!

Even as escaping the grip of the security blanket of our own bitterness and unforgiveness we cling to (the more we grip sin, the more it clings to us) can sometimes be so hard, in the same way breaking away from cherished traditions can be equally difficult as well. Christians today are overpowered by an influencing grip of fun and exciting Christmas traditions they enjoy that are hundreds of years older than they are. Some traditions are okay, while some are not God's desire. But strong memories of joy, laughter, and fun embedded in our own minds can make it hard to break away from anything that is not God's best for us. There is no condemnation; we are only presenting scriptures and sound rebuttals illuminating biblical truths, as a preacher would. This encourages Christians to increase their knowledge and grow their spiritual faith muscles so they may better trust in, obey, and more closely walk with God, thereby honoring Him the way He asked to be worshipped thousands of years ago!

There is no war against each other; only two different positions on a single topic. And there is no arguing with intention to fight one another; only a loving invitation to travel through another tough spiritual corridor to trust in God's word at all costs, renew the mind, and follow the Holy Spirit. On the other side of the door of faith and honor, we find exciting blessings God has in store for all His children.

2. DON'T JUDGE ME! CHRISTMAS IS NOT UNCLEAN

Worldly Argument:

Romans 14:13-14 says, "do not judge each other" and "nothing is unclean of itself." Therefore, no one should be judged for using a Christmas tree to worship God. Nothing is unclean of itself, and that includes the Christmas tree. Don't judge me.

Rebuttal:

After a careful examination of this whole chapter, we find this discussion in Romans 14 is NOT telling people to refrain from judging each other about Christmas trees. And Romans 14 is NOT including the Christmas tree in the 'nothing is unclean of itself' phrase, but rather this whole chapter is Paul simply being a referee between two groups of people (the meat eaters vs. the vegetarians) who are arguing with each other over which diet is the only diet God approves for spiritual holiness. In fact, Paul references "eating," "drinking," or "food" in this chapter eighteen times (if we understand the word "unclean" in verse 14 to be referencing unclean foods, then it's twenty-one times). As a referee, Paul is addressing the issue of eating foods that man considered clean vs. unclean among the believers.

Look what this passage says when you read it in proper context [*italics mine for clarity*] and add the next three verses! "(13) Therefore let's not judge one another any more [*over food*], but judge this rather, that no man put a stumbling block [*food issues*] in his brother's way, or an occasion for falling. (14) I know, and am persuaded in the Lord Jesus, that nothing [*food related*] is unclean of itself; except that to him who considers anything [*any food*] to be unclean, to him it is unclean. (15) Yet if because of food your brother is grieved, you walk no longer in love. Don't destroy with your food him for whom Christ died. (16) Then don't let your good be slandered, (17) for God's Kingdom is not eating and drinking, but righteousness, peace, and joy in the Holy Spirit" (Romans 14:13-17). Paul wraps up the full meaning of his fourteenth chapter by recapping in verse 20, "Don't overthrow God's work for food's sake." Romans 14 is only discussing food… nothing more.

Now let's talk about judging. We as brothers in Christ are not to judge each other in the form of pointing the finger of condemnation. Rather, we ARE commanded to judge each other in love, with a motive of building each other up and holding each other accountable as described in these verses:

- "He gave some to be apostles; and some, prophets; and some, evangelists,… (12) …to the building up of the body of Christ; (13) until we all attain to the unity of the faith,... to the measure of the stature of the fullness of Christ...; (15) but speaking truth in love, we may grow up in all things into Him, who is the head, Christ" (Ephesians 4:11-15).

- "For what have I to do with also judging those who are outside? Don't you judge those who are within? (13) But those who are outside, God judges... God judges outside the church body, but we judge within it." (1 Corinthians 5:12-13).
- "Brothers, even if a man is caught in some fault, you who are spiritual must restore such a one in a spirit of gentleness; looking to yourself so that you also aren't tempted." (Galatians 6:1).
- "Every scripture is God-breathed and profitable for teaching, for reproof, for correction, and for instruction in righteousness, (17) that the man of God may be complete, thoroughly equipped for every good work" (2 Timothy 3:16-17).

Finally, the phrase, "nothing is unclean of itself," in Romans 14 is NOT all encompassing. If it were, that would suggest lying is not 'unclean,' it is okay; murder is okay; adultery is okay, etc. Since we know these are all wrong in God's eyes, then the phrase "nothing is unclean of itself" is not all encompassing, and it cannot loosely give approval of the Christmas tree tradition.

3. AS LONG AS YOU'RE FULLY ASSURED IN YOUR MIND, WORSHIP HOWEVER YOU WISH

Worldly Argument:

Romans 14:5-6 says, "(5) One man esteems one day as more important. Another esteems every day alike. Let each man be fully assured in his own mind. (6) He who observes the day, observes it to the Lord; and he who does not observe the day, to the Lord he does not observe it…" So, if you're fully assured in your own mind that using a Christmas tree is alright with God, then use the tree to worship the Lord and there's no harm done!

Rebuttal:

Some suicide bombers are fully convinced in their own minds that their actions of mass murder will honor God. Just because someone is "fully convinced in his own mind" doesn't make it right. If God's own word specifically condemns an action you want to use as worship to Him, then Romans 14:5-6 cannot condone that which has already been condemned. This is not a free pass to worship God any way we choose EVEN IF YOU'RE "FULLY CONVINCED IN YOUR OWN MIND!"

Here are some examples of behaviors God condemns in the Bible:

- Burning or sacrificing children or people: CONDEMNED—Exodus 20:13; Deuteronomy 5:17
- Having sexual relations outside of marriage or with a partner of the same sex: CONDEMNED—Romans 1:26-28; Jude 1:5-8; 1 Timothy 1:8-11; 1 Corinthians 7:1-3; 1 Corinthians 6:9-11; Leviticus 18:22; Leviticus 20:13; Colossians 3:5
- Using God's name in vain, cussing, and telling dirty jokes: CONDEMNED—Exodus 20:7; Colossians 3:8; Ephesians 5:4; Ephesians 4:29-30; Proverbs 13:3; Psalm 141:3
- Lying: CONDEMNED—Leviticus 19:11; Psalm 119:163; Proverbs 12:22; Proverbs 13:5; Proverbs 17:7; Colossians 3:9; Revelation 22:15
- Murder/Killing others or suicide bombing those who don't share your faith: CONDEMNED—Exodus 20:13; Deuteronomy 5:17
- Using pagan worship traditions or tools (Asherah pole or tree) from other nations to

worship Jehovah: CONDEMNED—
Deuteronomy 12:30-31; Jeremiah 10:1-5

Man cannot burn children, commit adultery, cuss, lie, murder, or use idols and call it "worship" to Jehovah God. Man cannot worship or serve God in any manner they choose. They cannot break God's commandments as an act of worship toward Him just because their minds are fully convinced it would be okay. Worshipping God has its limits!

4. DO ALL IN THE NAME OF THE LORD

Worldly Argument:

1 Corinthians 10:31 says, "… whatever you do, do all to the glory of God." I want to worship God through Christmas traditions, so I can do it in the name of the Lord, or to the glory of God, right?

Rebuttal:

Again, this verse is just like the Romans 14 situation. Out of context and looking at only verse 31, it does seem to suggest the idea that "anything goes." However, in 1 Corinthians chapter 10, verses 19 through 33, Paul is explaining a food issue again. He is answering the question, "Is the food sold in the marketplace that has already been sacrificed to idols clean or unclean for believers to eat?" The phrase "whatever you do" in verse 31 is actually referring to whether you eat meat from the marketplace that was sacrificed to idols while it cooked OR whether you choose to avoid meat cooked on an idol's altar. So the phrase, "… whatever you do, do it all in the name of the Lord" is NOT an all-encompassing catch phrase and should not be used to justify all Christmas traditions any more than it should be used to justify suicide bombers to murder in the name of the Lord.

5. I CAN WORSHIP ANY WAY I WANT—GOD SEES MY HEART

Worldly Argument:

1 Samuel 16:7 says, "… For man looks at the outward appearance, but Yahweh looks at the heart." I can worship God any way I want because my heart has good intentions and God looks at my heart.

Rebuttal:

Taken out of context, this verse in 1 Samuel is all too easily interpreted to mean, "don't judge a man by what he does on the outside… praise him and tolerate his actions based on the intentions of his heart on the inside—that's what God does!" Or, simply put, "It doesn't matter what you do, only that you mean well." This fallible interpretation has been the unstable foundation for the demise of many a Christian and many a nation throughout history.

The bedrock of truth in this passage is that God was leading the prophet Samuel to find and anoint a young boy whose "spiritual heart" was already seeking after the "heart of God." Three chapters earlier, God revealed this in speaking to Saul, "But now your kingdom will not continue. Yahweh has sought for Himself a man [*seeking*] after His own heart, and Yahweh has appointed him to be prince over His people, because you have not kept that which Yahweh commanded you" (1Samuel 13:14). King Saul did not keep the commandment of God because Saul was seeking to please "Saul's" heart—not God's! In contrast, David wanted to lay his own heart's desires down to seek the things God's heart desires.

Jeremiah 17:9 teaches us, "The heart [*of man*] is deceitful above all things, and it is exceedingly corrupt: who can know it?" and Jeremiah 10:23 says, "Yahweh, I know that the way of man is not in himself: it is not in man who walks to direct his steps." A man's heart can lead him in a direction he thinks is right but can still be wrong in God's eyes. For example, a person may think, "I feel like my heart is telling me to embrace being gay… God made me that way." Just because God knows a man's heart, doesn't mean man can follow wherever his heart leads.

Following your own heart, no matter how sincere it may feel, can cause you to lose as much as an entire kingdom, or more. Yet, in exciting contrast, following the desires of God's heart can cause you to gain as much as an entire kingdom, or more!

6. DONATIONS INCREASE IN DECEMBER

Worldly Argument:

The percentage of benevolent giving and charitable donations soars around Christmastime. If you "take away" Christmas, people won't give as much anymore.

Rebuttal:

First, it is a ridiculously gross exaggeration to infer we could "take away" Christmas from the world as if a parent were taking away car privileges from a teenager. What we're doing is encouraging a heart that has been convicted to willingly lay something down for the purpose of honoring God. We are not taking anything away.

Second, to assume that "Christmas" is the only reason people donate doesn't really give God a whole lot of credit for being a strong influence of goodness and giving to widows, orphans, the poor, and the needy. Think about it!

Third, if a Christian loves God so much that he would lay down a lifelong tradition of a pagan holiday in order to honor his Lord and Savior, it is more than likely that his giving would increase to year-round benevolence, not decrease in December! In the book of Acts, the last part of chapter 2, we observe the early believers (the early Christians) selling their possessions and goods and distributing them among anyone in need. That's what naturally happens to a group of people overcome with the goodness of Christ overflowing out of their lives.

Don't ever let fear be the driving force of a decision. Fear is a tool of the devil to get us to react hastily in the wrong direction. We need to recognize that the thought, "If we lose Christmas, I FEAR giving percentages would go down," is only a message from Satan to drive us in the direction of keeping Santa, thereby keeping Deceit, keeping Distraction, and keeping Distortion in front of us all, so Jesus cannot rise to the top. The Devil wants to keep Jesus watered down. Don't let him trick you through fear!

7. BUT I LOVE CHRISTMAS

Worldly Argument:

I love sitting by a fireplace hung with stockings, drinking a cup of hot chocolate. I love the smell of a pipe while reading *'Twas the Night before Christmas* to the kids sitting next to a beautifully decorated Christmas tree. These things bring joy to me and create wonderful memories. Don't ask me to give it up because I love it… I love it ALL! Give me what I love! Give me what I want!

Rebuttal:

My most empathetic response is—they're right! Christmas can be exhilarating and exciting, and it can also be exactly like that coveted item the child sees in the grocery store. It can bring such good feelings to the child that when the parent says, "That is not the best of what I intended for you," then the child is willing to throw a tantrum of rebellion to obtain his own will rather than respectfully make a sacrifice to honor the will of his parent. This requires maturity and trust on the part of the child to say in his heart, "… not my will but yours be done" (Luke 22:42).

In this same way, there may be some who still want to worship God with a borrowed pagan tradition even after acknowledging that God hates being honored in this way. They are putting their own will before God's by essentially saying, "I don't have to let go of it because I love it". If you shared the truth with someone who is still in that mindset, don't belabor the issue. They're not ready for this yet, and that's okay. You planted the seed, and now the Holy Spirit can work on their heart in time—not you.

8. PAGANS STOLE CHRISTMAS FROM US!

Worldly Argument:

Pagans have always "stolen" things like trees, rocks, music, science, art, and sex, and perverted them. Christmas is no different. It was stolen from us when we were worshipping our God and the pagan nations tried to persuade us they had "beat us to the punch" on using trees in worship. Don't worry about what the pagans did with trees; you take it and do something good with it—enjoy it!

Rebuttal:

It is ludicrous, absurd, and outrageous to think, suggest, or try to convince anyone that Abraham, the Israelites, Moses, or any of God's chosen people were using a Christmas tree (or any tree) to worship or to celebrate the birth of Christ 2,000 years BEFORE Christ was ever born, when along came the pagan nations to "steal" the tradition away so they could worship their "sun god."

Pagan nations started this worship practice at least 1,500 years before Christ's birth. Spoiler Alert! We borrowed worshipping with trees from them. We put Christ's name on it. We deemed it a good thing. But God said in Deuteronomy He hates to be worshipped or honored in that way! So, inaccurately claiming that we did it first does not make it right.

9. THERE WAS A CHRISTMAS TREE IN GENESIS, and ALL TREES BELONG TO GOD… SO, CHRISTMAS TREES ARE GOOD.

Worldly Argument:

In conversations or debates, if the question arises "Where was there a Christmas tree in the Bible?" the Christmas defender replies, "Genesis. God made all trees at creation." He then argues his point by continuing with, "My Bible tells me in Psalm 24:1, 'The earth is Yahweh's, with its fullness; the world, and those who dwell therein.'" This argument implies that because every tree belongs to God, then automatically any use of a green tree (the Christmas tree) is scripturally approved.

Rebuttal:

For something to be scriptural, what do you need? Scripture! Combining biblical truth (Psalm 24:1) with someone's unscriptural desires (using a green tree as a tool to worship) can sound biblical, but watch out! Don't be fooled. Look at these statements that sound biblical (underlined portions are not scriptural) but fall short of sound doctrine:

- Our God is a loving God who loves EACH of us in our own individual ways, and He loves how we SEEK Him in our own individual ways.
- The Lord helps those who help themselves.
- Jesus said, "Love one another," and practice the virtue of tolerance with each other's differences.
- The earth is the Lord's and everything in it, even the Christmas tree.

The scripture *does* say, "Beloved, don't believe every spirit, but test the spirits, whether they are of God…" (1 John 4:1), and "For the weapons of our warfare are not of the flesh, but mighty before God… bringing every thought into captivity to the obedience of Christ" (2 Corinthians 10:4-5). Ideas, voices, thoughts, and influences come at us from all different directions and sometimes even from those we admire or trust: a church, a pastor, a famous celebrity, a friend, or even your heart. No matter where it comes from, it always needs to be verified with scripture. We can't just take things that sound biblical and immediately make them foundations for Christian decision-making without checking them thoroughly against God's word.

Yes, it is true the earth belongs to the Lord (Psalm 24:1). Yes, it is also true God said, "It is good," after all His creation in Genesis 1. However, the innate goodness of God's creations is entirely separate from the way man uses God's perfect creation. We cannot assume both the item and the use of the item are one and the same. A rock and a stick both created by God and declared good or sacred by God Himself could be constructed as an axe and unfortunately used by man as a murder weapon. The goodness of the rock and stick does not create instant scriptural endorsement of an act with those items which God has condemned. In the same manner, the established goodness of an evergreen tree does not grant instant scriptural endorsement of the use of that tree to engage in an act that God has directly condemned in Deuteronomy 12.

A perfect biblical example of this point I'm trying to make can be found in 1 Kings 14:22-23. "(22) Judah did that which was evil in Yahweh's sight, and they provoked Him to jealousy with their sins which they committed, above all that their fathers had done. (23) For they also built for themselves high places, sacred pillars, and

Asherah poles on every high hill and under every green tree."

Under the kingship of Rehoboam (King Solomon's son), the tribe of Judah used all these green trees (that, according to Psalm 24:1, belong to God) as tools of worship in the same way the nations before Israel did. In the next verse (verse 24) this is described as an abomination to God. It's not that God disliked the trees, but using the trees that belong to God for worshipping other gods made the Lord's anger burn. Now, when you consider God's command in Deuteronomy not to worship Him in the same way as other nations did, it's clear we cannot (nor could Rehoboam) use a tree as a tool to violate God, and then use Psalm 24:1 to justify that violation toward God.

King Rehoboam was not the only one who provoked God to anger through his misuse of trees. Read these passages of other occurrences where using trees for worship (sometimes even by God's chosen people) made God furious. Beginning back in Deuteronomy 12:2-3, God tells the Israelites to remove all worship spots under every green tree as they enter the Promised Land. God knows these trees, used as worship tools, are a small part of what will ensnare His people if they do not obey the Lord and completely remove them from the land. They don't. As a result, watch what happens:

Bible reference:	Consequence:
1 Kings 14:22-23	Rehoboam is king; Judah is defiled
2 Kings 16:4	Ahaz is king; Judah is defiled
2 Kings 17	Hoshea is king; Israel defiled; God rejects and afflicts Israel
Isaiah 57:5-13	Harlotry of Judah recounted; God will not hear their cries
Jeremiah 2:20-30	Israel is defiled; God strikes Israel
Jeremiah 3:1-6	Israel and Judah prostitute themselves; God withholds rains
Ezekiel 6:13	God condemns all Israel for idol worship (including use of green trees)

This is obviously a big deal to God for Him to make mention so many times throughout His Word. Please understand that I am not condemning you of worshipping other gods. My focus is more on explaining just how much God hates these worship practices and, in conjunction, just how much He despises being worshipped with the same tools and in the same manner as other gods!

Getting back on focus, when people say to you, "There was a Christmas tree in Genesis," that is a lie. There were trees created by God, but you cannot take that truth and stretch it into a lie that God made a Christmas tree. Also, when people tell you, "All the earth belongs to God," you cannot take that truth and stretch it into a blanket permission to take those things *created by* God and use them any way you see fit! God has clearly taught us how to worship Him, and how *not* to worship Him: never replicate pagan worship practices in His name! Those actions drive Him to anger and jealousy!

When God's truth gets blended with even a tiny bit of man's falsehood, it becomes impossible to use as solid foundation for moral decision-making. Make a habit of cross-referencing the things you hear or read (even from famous people, celebrities, preachers, or those you look up to) and make sure it all checks out with scripture. Test it against God's word no matter how reliable you think the source is. Last of all, once you check it against scripture, let God's word be the final authority over all the decisions you make.

10. WE NEED SANTA IN ORDER TO LEAD PEOPLE TO GOD

Worldly Argument:

Santa Claus is essential to spreading the gospel. Without Santa, it would be so difficult to explain the goodness of our God. When we get the opportunity to share our faith, here is what we can tell people:

We all know Santa Claus as an evolved story we tell our kids about a jolly old man in a red suit who lives in the North Pole, has magical powers, rides in a sleigh pulled by flying reindeer, and brings gifts to children around the world every Christmas Eve. But did you know that despite his stories of legend being changed and manipulated through exaggeration for over 1600 years, this fictitious character is used to try and capture the nature of goodness lived out by a real man named Nicholas who lived in the fourth century? He was the bishop of Myra from a town in what we know as modern-day Turkey. Nicholas, who was chosen as a member of the Nicene council, fervently defended the nature of Christ's equality to God. In one of these council meetings, he in fact slapped a man from Egypt named Arius for speaking heresy; he was leading a movement to denounce the triune nature of our God. After being reprimanded and stripped of his position for his actions, Nicholas was later reinstated as bishop. But because of his devout passion for serving the Lord and dedicating his life to blessing those in need, his deeds of giving generously to children and the poor led the people to eventually recognize him as Saint Nicholas. Overall, his life is a good example of how we should love and serve people the way God desires. Therefore, Santa Claus represents the essence of St. Nick, whose name was actually Nicholas, whose actions reflected the good character of the God I serve (with the exception of slapping people), thus allowing me to share with you now the good news of the gospel of Jesus Christ.

Rebuttal:

The spreading of the gospel would survive just fine without this weak leapfrog pitch as a case for God. If you want to effectively introduce and showcase the true character and immense love our God has for us, use John 3:16: "For God so loved the world, that He gave His one and only Son, that whoever believes in Him should not perish, but have eternal life." This short but rich verse is a fantastic place to start. It is straight from God; it directly reveals His character, His sacrifice, His love, His requirement for eternal life, and His promise. Plus, at one hundred and thirty-three characters with spaces, it tweets really well!

The message of God's eternal goodness is not compelled by the fantasy of Santa's continued existence. God and His message can stand on its own. We don't need Santa.

11. CHINESE FOOD ANALOGY

The previous ten samples of worldly arguments for the case of "saving Christmas" represent some reasonable examples you would expect to encounter in conversation. But what do you do when a more creative and elaborate presentation comes your way? Let's take a look at our last example.

Worldly Argument:

The following paraphrased and abbreviated argument came from a fantastic actor and a Christian I personally admire for many other reasons. He prepared this presentation and used a good British accent while wearing reading glasses as a prop to make his analogy come to life with a wonderfully comical sarcastic monologue. His speech began with an introduction in normal voice:

I want you to put on your "misguided fool" bifocals and follow along with me as I "act" educated and pretend to be very wise using a clever analogy and a British accent. (British accent and sarcasm begins) Dear friends, Chinese food is secretly threatening our churches today and should be rejected. It is a physical representation of the wickedly perverted Eastern philosophy of Monism, or "one-ness," that contradicts the trinity of our God. By combining rice, veggies, and chicken all together on one plate covered in sauces loaded with MONO-sodium glutamate, Chinese food seeks to subliminally undo the sacred characteristics that we so cherish in our God being three separate persons: the Father, the Son, and the Holy Ghost! Through the mixing of sweet and sour, we are also being led to participate in the unholy yin and yang concept. Dear friends, because the term 'Chinese food' is not found in the Bible, it is most assuredly NOT BIBLICAL and thus not for Christians to eat! And if you're eating Chinese food as a follower of Christ, well then, you're either turning a blind eye or you haven't been doing your research.

The actor takes off the prop glasses and speaks seriously to his audience, inferring that condemnation of Chinese food because the term 'Chinese food' is not found in the Bible is silly. He then articulates that misguided Christians are substituting the word "Christmas" in place of the word "Chinese food" from the silly argument above, and the result is causing confusion among the believers.

He implies that even though the Bible does not mention either of these terms, the Bible does not condemn them. Last, he invites the audience to participate in a call and response technique to bind together, in similar association, Chinese food with Christmas, so he can insinuate that if consuming Chinese food is good, then in the same manner, Christmas must be good too!

Rebuttal:

This Chinese food analogy skit uses cute sarcasm and is funny to listen to as a good actor brings a prepared monologue to life with comedy. But its point is made with unsound parallels, like comparing apples to broccoli! On the surface, the implication is that eating Chinese food and participating in Christmas to worship God are exactly the same. His argument strongly concludes that since the Bible mentions NOTHING about either, then it cannot condemn either. Therefore, since we find no condemnation, the bible (or God) indirectly allows our enjoyment of consuming Chinese food as strongly as He allows us to participate in Christmas and the use of the Christmas tree.

But the assumption that these two are similar cannot be more wrong. The Bible actually does mention both of these indirectly, AND with completely opposite views of each!

Romans 14:14 says, "I know, and am persuaded in the Lord Jesus, that nothing *(food related)* is unclean of itself;" [italics mine] thus proving all food, including Chinese food, is not unclean (or unholy) of itself—even though the exact wording of "Chinese food" is not printed in the Bible. Note: continuing with the lesson Paul gives in Romans 14, if your Christian brother feels in his conscience that consuming Chinese food may be something God disapproves of, then DO NOT eat it in front of him (even though there is nothing wrong with it) so that you do not cause your brother to stumble in his young and growing faith! So, Chinese food is indirectly mentioned in the Bible, and it is approved.

In opposing manner, taking borrowed traditions and tools of pagan worship to other gods, and worshipping Jehovah with those borrowed traditions and/or tools is ABSOLUTELY prohibited in Deuteronomy 12.

Christmas traditions were borrowed from the pagans and transformed to focus worship away from the sun god and toward Jesus; there's no getting around that fact. God condemns this practice, and even though the exact words "Christmas" or "Christmas tree" are not found in scripture, they are indirectly included in the condemnation because they are borrowed tools.

In conclusion, WE did not condemn Christmas because of its pagan origins; God condemned it because He said He hated being worshipped with a tradition that did not begin with Him! God has that authority and prerogative to do so. And as for Chinese food—nothing wrong with that at all. Please pass the orange chicken and another eggroll!

As we wrap up this chapter, when you engage in discussions about Christmas traditions you might be introduced to new ideas, perspectives, or views that come into question. Whether it is a simple view or even an elaborate and creative interpretation, I encourage you to always go back to the basics of God's word. Ask God what He thinks about it. His precepts are timeless, foundationally solid, and reliable for addressing any uncertainty. Find the basic fundamental concepts in question, then take it to God, take it slow, and filter them through His word and let God's position be your final authority to settle any matter. You will also find this approach works for any topic, and any situation you encounter throughout your life, not just Christmas!

- CHAPTER 14 -

TO TREE, OR NOT TO TREE? THAT IS THE QUESTION

If you've decided to follow in the footsteps of Gideon and remove the "Asherah pole" in your house by taking down the tree, I want to applaud and encourage you. It's a tough thing to take the road less traveled and move in a direction of faith with the intention of honoring God, but I guarantee you will not be disappointed when the blessings He promised start increasing!

"So, what do I do now?" you may ask. I can share with you some ideas from our family; however, do not think your family has to do exactly what my family does. Since you are now convinced that God says not to use a tree and not to lie, moving forward, your house and family traditions will look different than they used to. But, through this conviction and change, your new family traditions will continue to make great memories with happiness, joy, and laughter, maybe even more so than before… the only difference is there won't be a tree or stories of Santa involved.

At the beginning of this book, I asked the question, "How is a Christian home supposed to look different during Christmas?" I do have to bust the doors wide open and reveal that this is not an issue of looking or acting a certain way only during the Christmas holidays. This is truly about living a certain way all year round. A Christian home should look like the image you were created in. Your home will look like God, the Holy Spirit, and Jesus all wrapped up in one.

As your family continues to strive toward achieving a truly godly home, keep in mind that change can be slow, and we are still only human. On some days, the feeling of the Holy Spirit might not be felt as much as usual. And at other times, the essence of who Jesus is will flow freely through your words and actions. Overall, the three elements of the Godhead will start to consume the behavior of you and your family, and soon your home won't look like the world—it will look quite different. That's what you want! You want the opportunity for others to ask the question, "What is it that is so different about the way you do things? How do I get what you've got?" Boom! Now you can tell them about the crazy goodness of how God honors those faithful to Him, faithful to His leading, and faithful to His Word!

Take a look with me at a suggested blueprint for a Christian home all year round:

✞ A CHRISTIAN HOME SHOULD LOOK LIKE GOD

First, God is holy. Nothing outside of Him makes Him holy, He just IS. It's kind of like when He said, "I am who I am" (Exodus 3:14). He is holy because He IS holy. This may be a little hard to understand in the raw, but here's what I'm getting at. God IS good because "goodness" is His makeup. God is not good because some outside person, being, or force judged His performance and awarded Him this distinction with a medal. Therefore, the actions He takes and the decisions He makes are always good, always righteous, and always holy because they come from the source of His being or existence.

1 Peter 1:14-16 says, "(14)… not conforming yourselves according to your former lusts (meaning the desire to follow what the world is doing or what feels good to you), as in your ignorance; (15) but just as He who called you is holy, you yourselves also be holy in all of your behavior, (16) because it is written, "You shall be holy; for I am holy." Here, Peter is referencing Leviticus 11:44-45, Leviticus 19:2, and Leviticus 20:7, and it also

coincides with Matthew 5:48 where Jesus tells us to be "perfect."

So, to be holy with all our behavior (not just our holiday-time behavior), we should firmly (with no exceptions) be rooting all our decisions all year in holiness, not based off of "I'll just do the lesser of two evils," or "I'll go this way because it can't be all that bad," or "It's probably okay because a lot of good people are doing it."

When God makes decisions, they are NOT based off outside influences. God's decisions are rooted in His existence of absolute perfection, not majority rule. Since we as humans are not rooted in perfect goodness (Psalm 51:5; Eph. 2:2-3), there is no way to be holy without God. We need to tap into God's holiness in order to be holy and to make decisions for holy behaviors. The Holy Spirit can funnel God's desire and His will directly to us, to help us accomplish any task, but in the end, we must voluntarily make right decisions to manifest God's holiness in our own behavior.

So, what are some examples of making firm decisions for living based on holiness alone? Some of you may want to buckle in tight and hold on to your seats. A few of these simple examples are topics for whole books, and while some may seem like radical examples, keep in mind that when you make radical decisions for God's namesake, He manifests radical blessings on your behalf (that is His pleasure)! Here we go.

- I will keep the Sabbath Holy. I will work six days a week and rest (do no business stuff) for one day in order to honor God's commandment and honor Him (Exodus 20:8-11).
- I will not watch horror films, go to a haunted house, or purposefully make myself scared, because the word of God is explicitly clear that I am not to fear. Purposefully bringing fear into my life unequivocally contradicts the will of what God desires in my life—His desire for peace in all of my being (2 Timothy 1:7; Isaiah 41:10; Philippians 4:6-7; 1 John 4:18; Psalm 23:4).
- No matter what friends, relatives, or any other people do, I will never hold grudges or execute revengeful actions on someone who hurts me. Instead, I will bless those who curse me, do good to those who hate me, and pray for people who spitefully hurt me, knowing that blessing those who hurt me renders blessings on me! (Matthew 5:44; 1 Peter 3:9; Romans 12:17; Romans 12:19).
- I will not be disrespectful to God or set an example of disrespect for my children to see by leaving church early to make it home in time for the Superbowl (Matthew 22:37).
- I will not gossip or even participate as a listener in other people's gossip. I will either speak up and stop the group, or I will leave (Psalm 101:5).

- I will never support the actions or initiatives of a gay/lesbian philosophy. I will also speak out against it in a loving way. We can love the people but not tolerate sin around us or our children (Leviticus 18:22; 20:13; Romans 1:18-32; 1 Corinthians 6:9-10; 1 Timothy 1:8-10).
- I will tithe; even when I feel like I am in poverty (Matt. 23:23; Luke 11:42, 2 Corinthians 9:7).
- I will choose to speak only positive things about a person or say nothing until I can (Ephesians 4:29).
- I will never entertain a thought of adultery or seek other outlets to solve unmet intimacy needs. This is a sin against God, it is dishonoring and sinful against my spouse, it is sinful against my own body, and it destroys the family (Matthew 5:27-28; Proverbs 6:23-29; 1 Corinthians 6:18).
- I will be patient with my children. The nature of God's love, grace, and patience needs to be demonstrated through my actions and character (Ephesians 6:4).
- I will not cuss or use foul language (Colossians 3:8; Matthew 12:36-37).
- I will not worship my God using pagan worship tools or rituals because He abhors it and He commanded me not to (Deuteronomy 12:29-31).

These are just some examples. Some may seem obvious, while others may seem extreme, but they are all deeply rooted in the word of God. And oh, by the way—even as the writer of this book, many of those examples I gave are things I have been guilty of in my past and still fall short of today, but I'm still working on them. You cannot expect to change overnight… but you should try. However, if you ever follow through with a decision you know is in direct opposition to the leading of the Holy Spirit or the word of God, then you are purposefully making the choice *not* to be godly. It all boils down to this: we need to consistently strive to make the atmosphere in our homes reflect the nature of the God who loves us.

✞ A CHRISTIAN HOME SHOULD UTILIZE THE WISDOM OF THE HOLY SPIRIT

Next, begin filling the home with the Holy Spirit. Let God lead you and your home through this new way of worshipping Him by listening to the Holy Spirit and letting Him guide you through every decision, no matter how great or small. If you don't know how to listen to the Holy Spirit, here is a short crash course:

- Understand and have confidence that the Holy Spirit will NEVER contradict God's word (the Bible). So, get into the word of God. Read your Bible often. Look up as many passages and scriptures as you can find concerning the decision you're wrestling with. When you plant one hundred seeds of God's word in your mind, thoughts, and meditations, the Holy Spirit can then use the harvest of what you planted to talk to you and reveal His direction for you with much more clarity.

- Quiet yourself and avoid the noise of the world. Satan wants to clutter your mind with too much radio, too many TV shows and movies, too many activities, too many errands, and way too much social media... all to keep you from hearing the quiet voice or the leading of the Holy Spirit. Force yourself to make time to get away from the rush, anxiety, and worry, and find your way to a place where you can physically experience the scripture. "Be still and know that I am God" (Psalm 46:10). That is the best way to hear the Holy Spirit.

- Listen and decipher. You must understand that there are two voices constantly calling out trying to get your attention. Proverbs calls them Wisdom and Folly (Proverbs 1:20; Proverbs 8). Another way to classify these two voices is as "The Voice of God" and "The Voice of Satan." The voice of God is the Holy Spirit, and it speaks to you calmly in peace, assurance, forgiveness, selflessness, and love. Satan speaks through fear, condemnation, revenge, and hatefulness, and the message is usually self-serving.

The biggest thing you have to watch out for is Satan convincing you that he doesn't really talk to you. If you believe that every voice in your heart and mind comes only from God, Satan can do a lot of talking and a great deal of damage, making you think you're listening to and following God. Listen for the voices, but know there are two.

- Test the spirits. The fact that God commands us to test the spirits (1 John 4:1) is another validation that some spirit voices are not the ones we should be listening to or following. If you don't know which voice is which inside your head (heart), you must test their messages against the word of God. Remember, the voice of God (the Holy Spirit) will never contradict His written word. This is another reason to be reading your Bible constantly. If you can find multiple scriptures to support the feelings or promptings you're hearing, it's a good bet you're headed in the right direction. But if the message you get from reading His word consistently causes friction with the voice in your head or heart, be cautious and prudent before you act on that voice or feeling. With a solid foundation of truth from reading the word of God frequently, testing the spirits becomes a much easier task.

- Follow the peace. Before you make a decision between two options, meditate. When you meditate on a single possible decision and imagine following through with it, the peace of God will settle on the right decision, whereas unease will churn in your belly when you meditate on the wrong decision.

- If you still are not sure what to do in a matter after doing your best to read, be still, listen, and meditate, resisting the urge to make a decision out of your own impatience. Just pause. God is patient, and He will not punish you for being slow if you are sincerely and diligently seeking His word or His guidance in a matter. The devil operates in the opposite manner, signaling, "Rush, rush, rush. Hurry up and make a decision or you're gonna miss it!" Take your time—God is patient.

You should not alter your Christmas traditions blindly just because I or someone else suggests it, or because someone you admire does it, or because it is the next big Christian fad. You must let the Holy Spirit be your guide throughout this decision (as it should be for all other decisions in your life). Allowing the Holy Spirit to guide you and your family in these moments of change will give your home a calming peace, and you cannot go wrong.

✞ A CHRISTIAN HOME SHOULD LOOK LIKE CHRIST

Lastly, to have a home that looks like Christ, observe the characteristics of Jesus and copy those. In Luke 14:12-14, Jesus tells us to bless those who cannot repay us. So, look for and jump at any opportunities that allow you to bless individuals who could never possibly pay you back for the kindness you show.

Everywhere Jesus went, He was telling people about the Kingdom of God and freeing those from the bondage of Satan's grip (Luke 13:16). When you find yourself in blessing opportunities or even just conversations with new people, share the good news about God. Spreading the gospel message is a command given by Jesus. This is referred to as the Great Commission found in Matthew 28:18-20. Talk to people as they come into your path and share the freeing hope of the gospel and what Jesus has done for them!

Jesus was constantly talking to His Father in prayer. Don't be afraid to ask people if they want or need prayer. If they say yes, you can be bold and lay hands on them while you pray with compassion in your heart and confidence in your request to God (Mark 11:24; Hebrews 4:16).

Jesus washed His disciples' feet and told us to do the same. I'm not saying you need to start a pedicure business, but even if you don't have a gift to give, you and your family can look for ways to be of service to others. Cook and deliver a meal, mow a lawn, help clean a house, run errands for someone who could use the help. Be creative. Be a servant.

Christ did not come to condemn the world (John 3:17). It's easy to turn a blind eye to the man on the street holding a sign that reads, "NEED HELP, GOD BLESS" but try not to pass judgement or withhold from him assuming he'll probably just buy booze. Remember, it is the goodness of God that leads men to repentance. You can always ask him if he is hungry, make a U-turn, buy him a value meal, and drop it off with a smile of God's mercy. When it comes to mercy, the people who deserve it the least need it the most.

Jesus said, I only do what my Father shows me to do (John 5:19). I've given you just a few ideas of how you can emulate Christ in your home around the Christmas holidays, but always be ready to do what the Father shows you to do. Jesus didn't argue when His dad moved Him to go spit in a blind man's eyes. In your home, trust your Father's promptings no matter how crazy it may sound; there may just be a miracle about to happen!

- CHAPTER 15 -

TESTIMONY, IDEAS, AND A VISION

Why did our family make the switch? Well, it didn't happen overnight, but it did start with a simple question. Let me share from the beginning how and why my wife Rachelle influenced our family to transition away from some of the common Christmas traditions of the culture and make a move closer to God. I can recall three separate phases that all just came together.

❖ Phase I: It's a lie!

When our kids were young, the Holy Spirit dropped a thought into my wife's head. She had a feeling that telling the kids about Santa was not truthful. She came to me and shared this concern. I arrogantly brushed it off, justifying that it was okay to tell harmless, joy-filled, innocent white lies because, after all, it was Santa Claus and he was good fun for young kids. My attitude at the time was, "If it's fun for the kids, it's good for the kids." You don't mess with traditions older than yourself, and you certainly don't take away a tradition that involves fun for the kids! Quietly under my pride I couldn't help but think, "Rachelle's right, lying is lying no matter the size." For years this spiritual nagging increased in me and kept growing more and more in Rachelle, too. The seed of questioning the need to lie to our kids about Santa had been planted and was growing.

❖ Phase II: What's the meaning of all this?

A few years later, I was paralyzed from a bicycle accident. As I was released from the hospital in the fall of 2009, Rachelle was instantly responsible for all the care of an immobile paralytic and three young children, Avery, Kara, and Samuel. She was overwhelmed to say the least as we both lost our income potential as she was the physical life-blood of the whole family.

Approaching the holidays, the local police department, a benevolent law firm, and another church all separately wanted to make our family the primary focus of their Christmastime blessing outreach efforts. At that time, we were barely getting by in a small two-bedroom apartment paid for by donations from our church and friends. Avery, our oldest, responsible and trustworthy had been thrust unwillingly into a world of being mom's little helper for too many things. Before, she liked to play dress-up and pretend to be grown up, but now she had to actually be grown up more than a seven year-old should just so that our whole family could make it through the mundane events of long and tough days. Avery did it with a servant heart. Kara, our heartwarming little gem of a girl, willingly to play the part of nurse alongside mom (sporting blue hospital gloves three sizes larger than her precious five year-old fingers), was consistently willing to do anything to help her daddy heal. At less than one year old, Samuel had no idea how his life had just changed but his boyish curiosity for the beeping buttons on dad's power wheelchair and his loud infectious laugh kept us going when times were tough.

Even though my hospital bed and equipment was taking up most of the space in the living room, we still had enough room to set up a small Christmas tree and celebrate what we did have… each other. For parents who desired to bless such wonderful and deserving children for Christmas, the generosity of these three groups felt like a welcome blessing from God.

When all the gifts finally arrived, it was like a scene out of the movies. Presents were piled under the tree, around the floor, along the walls, on top of the couch, in the windows; it was truly an overwhelming sight to see.

Interestingly, a lot of those presents were labeled "from Santa." Of course, we told our kids God was the one blessing us, but why did Santa's name have to be on God's blessings? After that day of engulfing favor, it felt like we were all alone, stranded on a deserted island of Christmas presents. It was as if when the good deed was done with a smile and a cheerful heart, people checked us off the list. This year's "jewel in their heavenly crown" had been earned, but it was time for them all to move on. At that moment, a second seed (a very large seed) had just been planted. This time it was questioning the real meaning of a holiday we call Christmas.

What was it about Christmas that brought out such willingness from a surplus of kind hearts to give financially, to donate the time to wrap so many presents, and to spend a day delivering or presenting all of the gifts just to have the goodwill volunteers seemingly fall off the face of the earth, never to be heard from again once the seasonal holiday passed at the turn of the calendar? Did they not know that, although the presents were an amazing gesture of goodwill, inwardly we were crying out for daily help just to survive?

❖ Phase III: Excess

The next big Holy Spirit moment occurred when we were opening all those presents, given by the three benevolent groups. In previous Christmas Day experiences, we would open gifts one at a time, with each person being the focus of the full family's attention and support. We could all experience the joy with one another and for one another. But now there were so many gifts, when we started with each child opening one present at a time, we quickly realized the sun might go down before we finished. What ended up happening was all the kids dove into a frenzy of opening all "their own" presents independently, as fast as they could, which left the family participation and appreciation in the dust.

Another notable difference this year was, while the past had lent itself to opening each present, taking it out of its packaging, admiring and cherishing the gift, saying "thank you" to the giver, etc., in this instance, after the unwrapping ceremonies had ended, three small mountains of unboxed and unappreciated toys remained on the floor, still bound in their retail packaging. It took us weeks to unbox each gift, read the instructions, assemble parts, insert batteries, break down and throw the packaging away, and play with every toy. By the time we finished, there were so many toys that many of them had already been forgotten. Our family had just experienced a small glimpse of what comes with excess.

Within a few years, ideation and implication of these three phases started to culminate even more in our hearts and in our spirits and eventually motivated us to take a different direction:

- Santa is a lie
- What's the meaning of all this?
- Experiencing excess

My wife Rachelle was taking an evening class at church, and the Holy Spirit prompted her again on the whole Christmas issue. She came home and shared that prompting with me, and we meditated on it. Now, in the past, my decisions would be influenced by my own internal questioning: "When I was a kid, what did my family always do for Christmas?" and, "What seems to be the majority rule of Christmas traditions among Christians today?" But when Rachelle shared her prompting this time and we were digging into the word of God with the mindset of "What does God say about this?" it became clearer and clearer that Christmas, as a whole, was not exhibiting the true nature of God. This realization was bothering us, and we didn't want to be a part of it anymore.

It was the patient urging of the Spirit on my wife's heart which triggered further study on my part. The intention of creating a two-paragraph response to Rachelle morphed into two pages, two chapters, and eventually two years! During that process, our family changed a few Christmastime habits for the better. Now, by writing this book, it is my goal to share the steps of spiritual growth and blessings our family has received and lead others in the same direction so they too can experience a new level of the goodness of our God!

You can let the Holy Spirit lead you in becoming a leader in the world too. Being a leader can inspire change. Consider this vision: if even more Christians, through this topic of Christmas, follow our lead and eventually create a habit of obeying God's promptings no matter the cost, it could very well change our nation's overall relationship with God… ultimately releasing an entire nation from oppression. You might ask in a sarcastic or doubtful way, "Can you seriously suggest that simply changing a habit of worship in December could completely relieve a nation of oppression?!"

My unyielding answer is ABSOLUTELY! YES! Go back and read Gideon's story in Judges. That is exactly what happened to a nation—God's nation, the Israelites. When Gideon as in individual put God first and tore down the altar and Asherah pole, what happened? God fought for His people and released them from their oppression. God has not changed, and when God fights FOR you, you NEVER lose!

By the way, if you don't think we are in a situation of oppression, you're living in a world with your eyes closed and your ears plugged! Depression, suicide, divorce, disease, drug overdosing, abortions, same-sex marriage, self-centeredness, self-reliance… (and a lot of this ridiculous nonsense is in the church!) can all be dramatically reduced by putting God and Jesus in the right place in our minds and habits! Putting God and Jesus in their rightful place doesn't have to begin as a New Year's Resolution; we can start any time of year and continue through the next eleven months! Imagine what would happen if God started fighting for us like he did with Gideon. Then, we can watch God heal our entire nation. YES, IT IS POSSIBLE. With God, all things are possible.

VISUALIZE THE POSSIBILITIES

Here's a small vision of conceivable healing within a nation. eMarketer reports the U.S. spent $998.32 Billion dollars during the 2018 holiday season. Imagine all that money we pour into Christmas shopping being re-routed to bless the poor, the widows, and the needy! Instead of 100%, think more realistically with me. If we as Christians (75% of the U.S. population) in this nation re-routed only 5% of our Christmas spending and gave that money to our churches or benevolent groups, then an additional $37.4 billion dollars a year would be going to help orphanages, widows, and those in need! What would this look like in tangible action rather than one giant dollar report? It is estimated that the United States has 400,000 children in foster care with 100,000 of those waiting to be adopted. The average age of a child in foster care is 8-9 years old, which means we can invest in their lives for 9 years before they turn 18. If only 5% of U.S. Christian holiday spending was re-routed to these children alone, here's what could happen EVERY SINGLE YEAR:

- ✓ $15,000 for every child could be given to foster parents to reimburse for food and clothing expenses.
- ✓ $8,000 for every child could be given to foster parents to reimburse for medical insurance premium expenses.
- ✓ $5,000 for every child could be given to foster parents to reimburse for family vacation—encouraging them to invest in making good family memories through travel.
- ✓ $4,000 for every child could be given to foster parents to reimburse for school activities or participation in extra-curricular expenses.
- ✓ $1,000 for every child could be deposited each year for nine years to be used for a $9,000 wedding fund after they turn eighteen years old.
- ✓ $2,000 for every child could be deposited each year for nine years to be used for the purchase of an $18,000 vehicle (pre-owned of course) after they turn eighteen years old.
- ✓ $26,000 for every child could be deposited each year for nine years totaling just over a QUARTER of a MILLION dollars for college when they turn eighteen years old.

Yes, changing our habits could make a HUGE difference. The listed figures only account for 5% of the Christian population, but what if it was more? Some of us could give up not only Christmas presents, but birthday presents too. This could most assuredly be done! You do the math!

SUGGESTIONS TO GUIDE YOU THROUGH THE CHANGE

Here are some family conversation starter ideas for introducing the new direction of change for a family (especially with children):

1. Start with the basics: We're going to do a Bible study on lying.
    a. Scripture reading – Leviticus 19:11; Proverbs 12:22, John 8:44; Colossians 3:9
    b. Prayer – "God help us not to lie for any reason at all, even little white lies we think are innocent."
    c. Discussion questions
        i. Who is the "Father of Lies"?
        ii. What kind of lies does he want us to tell?
        iii. If we ever catch ourselves lying, what should we do?
    d. Confession time with Mom and Dad
        i. Dad and Mom confess lies about Santa
        ii. Dad and Mom ask for forgiveness

iii. Commit to being a family that tells the truth from now on about all things.

2. Family story time – Gideon
   a. Scripture reading – Judges chapters 6-7
   b. Prayer – "God, bless us with the courage to honor you the way you want to be honored, just like Gideon. And bless us that we can be a part of great miracles you have coming up."
   c. Discussion questions
      i. What did God ask Gideon to do in chapter 6 verses 25-26?
      ii. Why do you think God asked Gideon to do this before he went into battle with only 300 good guys against 120,000 bad guys?
      iii. If God asked you to honor Him a certain way, would you want to do it?
   d. Discovery and connection time with Mom and Dad
      i. Read Deuteronomy 12:29-31. Explain: God doesn't want us to worship Him using the same tools or methods that pagan (ungodly) people

used to worship their gods. Our God HATES that!

ii. Read 1 Kings 14:22-26. Explain: God HATED that trees were used as tools to worship other gods. It made Him so angry, He disciplined His chosen people for doing it.

iii. Connect the two above: If God disciplined His people for using trees as worship tools, and He says not to worship Him using the same tools, then we shouldn't be using a tree to worship Him.

e. Make a family commitment

i. Let's find other ways as a family to worship God that please Him because we love Him.

3. Family story time – "God is so cool; Don't steal His honor"

a. Scripture Reading – Matthew 6:8; Luke 12:7; Psalm 33:13-15; Jeremiah 23:23-24; Proverbs 15:3 (knows when sleeping, awake, number of hairs on head); John 15:7; Luke 12:32; Psalm 35:27 (giver of good things); Matthew 19:26 (nothing's impossible);

Romans 1:17; Galatians 3:11; Hebrews 10:38 (who should we believe)

b. Prayer – "God, help us to understand that you love us so much. You see and hear everything we do. You want to protect us and bring us good things because you love us so much. Help us to be careful not to put anyone else in your position or give anyone else honor or praise for the things you do."
c. Discussion questions
    i. Who knows when we are sleeping and when we're awake? What else does He know?
    ii. What does God like to give us?
    iii. What magical or miraculous things can you imagine God can do?
    iv. Can anybody else do what our God can do?
    v. If you (children) did amazing things that made us proud, how would you feel if we threw a party for someone else and celebrated them for what you accomplished (even though they didn't actually do the things you did so well)?

vi. Should we be celebrating and honoring Santa for doing the things God has done?

d. Make a family commitment

i. Let's give God all honor for what He has done. No more Santa.

IDEAS FOR CHRISTMASTIME ACTIVITIES, FUN, AND THANKFULNESS

Please don't fall into the idea or fear that if you remove Santa or the Christmas tree there is no more fun to be had. That's why the Christmas defender wants to label us as "bah humbuggers" who just want to throw a "wet blanket" over Christmas and "steal all the fun out of the season." Not so! There is loads of fun to have this time of year. So get out there, live it up, and praise God while you're at it. Now that the tree is gone, you can simply replace the old traditions with some new ones. Here are some ideas that will not only create more family bonding time and bring you closer to one another, but will become God-growing moments as well.

- Snowflake Tradition

Sit around the table as a family to fold and cut snowflakes, talk, laugh, giggle, and bond. Discuss how no two snowflakes in the world are alike and how great God is that He knows every single one. Enjoy time together hanging them up, admiring each child for his/her own creativity. When you take them down, sign, date, and laminate each one. When the next year comes around, hang the past snowflakes up first around the house before repeating the next family snowflake-making night. Sign, date, laminate, and keep repeating the process. Look ahead and envision the future. Talk about how many snowflakes you're going to have when the grandkids come to visit and participate. For an even more memorable effect, write something you are thankful for on each snowflake; in ten years, you will have quite a collection of memories.

- Thankful Wall Poster

God loves to be thanked, but even more than that, He knows that when we give Him thanks, it is good for us! Giving thanks to God, while it honors Him, doesn't change God, but it does increase our knowledge, confidence, and re-assurance of how good a God He is, and that makes us stronger! So, on Thanksgiving Day, hang up or display a "Thankful Poster" with a pen and encourage everyone to sign it as they would a guest book at a wedding. Everyone can sign it as many times as they want with as many "thankfuls" as they want. Date it, frame it, and display it wherever and however you'd like. Do one for each year.

- Read the book of Esther

If you would like a good reason to give gifts to each other, Esther may be a good way to do it. Divide these ten chapters up however you like and enjoy reading and discussing one of the most exciting "twist ending" true stories the Bible has to offer! In reading this book, we find that Esther plays a big part in saving all the Jews from imminent death. But a unique part is at the end of the story, when her father Mordecai gains such a high position, then commands all the Jews who are spread throughout 127 nations to start, and keep for all generations, a new annual tradition. That new tradition, called Purim, would commemorate God's mighty protective right hand turning near-annihilation into a rally of strength for all of God's people—all while they were in the middle of captivity! Even though this celebration was to be done and remembered in our months of late February/early March, we can still celebrate God's goodness any time of year. Part of this celebration is God's people giving gifts to one another in remembrance of how He saved them, so now you can use the giving of a gift to bring up the conversation of celebrating God's protection for His people instead of passing it off as, "It's a gift from Santa Claus."

- Read the story of Gideon

As I suggested above, the true story of Gideon is only two chapters (Judges 6 and 7) and a fun read for all ages! Use it as a segue into why we want to do away with the tree BUT STILL WORSHIP GOD, or use it as a reminder each year as to why it is valuable to stand strong for God in the face of opposition (even if that opposition is from people you know and care about).

- Family Game Night
  Whether it be card games, board games, charades, Twister, or any other game, get together as a family and make memories with smiles, laughing, snuggling, and just plain fun.

- Christmas Lights
  Grab some flashy lights and decorate your house inside, outside, or both if you like. Also, there's nothing like piling in a car with friends or family and going to look at Christmas lights.

- Manger Scene
  Since I suggested lights in the yard, go ahead and enjoy the fun of assembling a manger scene. I discussed earlier that God mentions the commemoration of Jesus' death and resurrection with much more power and emphasis than His birth, but if you want to praise our God for sending baby Jesus, by all means do so; just don't include the worship tree as a part of honoring Him.

- Feasting

  God lists seven "Holy Feasts" throughout the year where the people of God assemble and remind themselves of God's promises and wonders. He knows that fellowship is associated with feasting. In no way am I insinuating that Thanksgiving turkey and a Christmas ham are to replace God's "Holy Feasts," but I am saying that while you're together feasting, enjoy the fellowship and use that time to acknowledge, thank, or praise God (and not just focus all our time on things like football).

INVITED TO PUBLIC GATHERINGS? WHAT TO DO?

How do we handle invitations to Christmas parties? My answer: I have no absolutes as a single answer for all party invitations or every situation. But here are a few thoughts to consider.

We know that Jesus ate with sinners (Mark 2:13-17). We also know that Jesus never sinned (1Peter 2:21-23). Therefore, we can at least deduce two solid conclusions:

1. First, Jesus did not commit a sinful act or wrongdoing in His father's eyes while fellowshipping with sinners at a party.

2. Second, Jesus never sinned even by *attending* a party.

As we continue to discuss this question, I do not want to imply that anyone should look at or label Christmas party-goers as "sinners." We are ALL sinners. When reading about Mary, Martha, the apostles, disciples, followers of Jesus, the wedding party, the tax collectors, and everyone else Jesus fellowshipped with, we know that they were ALL sinners too! We need to keep in mind that it is the love and kindness of God (Christ) that leads men to repentance (Romans 2:4). Imagine the many moments of love and kindness Jesus created through fellowship and/or bonding with all those He "partied" or feasted with.

What I would like us to do is view a Christmas party at work, school, neighborhood, church building, or wherever it may be as an opportunity to create bonds of trust and love. Selflessly talk to people, get to know them, and ask them questions about their lives. Build a relationship no matter how small. Jesus knew when He entered a party, many of the partygoers lacked the INFORMATION needed to be set free. But He also knew it might only take a tiny relationship established at the party to open the door to someone's heart so they could hear the message Jesus wanted to share the next day!

It is likely someone at the party might ask you the question, "When does your family put the tree up?" Yes!

That right there could be the opportunity to introduce and share your new tradition. A word of caution, though: share slowly in "bite size" morsels, unless they are asking for more. For example:

HARRY: My kids are so excited about Christmas, they begged me and their mother to let them put the tree up on Thanksgiving Day. How about you guys, when do you pull out the old pine tree from the attic?

TOM: [confidently] We don't put the tree up at all anymore!

HARRY: What? Do you mean not at all?

TOM: Yep, we got rid of it two years ago… we don't even use a tree anymore.

HARRY: Why?

TOM: We learned that God hates it, and we don't want to do anything that dishonors Him.

HARRY: Where in the world did you hear that?

TOM: God actually wrote it in the Bible. I didn't believe it until I saw it. Liz and I had no idea it was there, but when we read it, it was more than obvious.

HARRY: What was there? And where were you reading?

In short, a Christmas party could be just the place to be friendly and let the Holy Spirit bring you the right person at the right time to share what you've discovered. You don't have to condemn friends who don't know this information yet or point a finger of chastisement. Just consider how Jesus might mingle and be ready to give a soft answer when His father brings Him an inquiring sheep. Show up for God and wait for His signal, and He can use you in a mighty way.

As always, use discretion and ask the Holy Spirit to guide you in choosing which Christmas events to attend and/or participate in. Do not commit to or attend any event where you know temptation of certain activities could cause you to sin! King David would inquire God's approval before going into battle… you do the same.

ENCOURAGEMENT TO YOU

Moving forward, if you ever feel like you're receiving opposition from other Christians, family members, or friends, hang on to these nuggets of truth:

1. "Everyone who has left houses, or brothers, or sisters, or father, or mother, or wife, or children, or lands, for my name's sake, will receive one hundred times, and will inherit eternal life" (Matthew 19:29). Choosing to take the path that follows in the footsteps of Gideon means you will be leaving behind some traditions that

have had lifelong ties and memories. By all means, keep those happy memories of smiles, warm feelings, and times spent with loved ones! We're not discarding the wonderful memories you have built up, but we're simply choosing not to let the Christmas tree be a part of worship to Jesus and God as we move forward. We can worship and honor God in so many ways that can make lasting memories for you and your generations that follow. Breaking ties and leaving behind lifelong and cherished traditions is just like leaving family behind to follow God (Abram did it and look how God changed his life dramatically), and the promise from God in Matthew 19:29 to reward you one hundred times is something you can count on.

2. "But even if you should suffer for righteousness' sake, you are blessed" (1 Peter 3:14). Since you are guaranteed to receive a reward for taking the heat of verbal persecution while doing something to bring honor to God, then don't give up or give in when people call you crazy—reward is guaranteed and imminent!

3. "But sanctify the Lord God in your hearts; and always be ready to give an answer to everyone who asks you a reason concerning the hope that is in you, with humility and fear" (1 Peter 3:15). Understand how blessed you

are to be in this position of "controversy and curiosity." When you stand out for God (being light in a dark world), people take notice! When you take this stand to lay down Christmas for Christ, controversy will usually come from other Christians, and curiosity will come mostly from the world. Whether it comes from other Christians or those who don't know Christ yet, be ready to give your answer for the faith you exercise. Because when they ask "Why?" about your anti-Christmas tree position, your confident, readied answer will bring honor and glory to God and could very well be the seed that eventually leads a soul to God as well!

4. "But some Jews from Antioch and Iconium came there, and having persuaded the multitudes, they stoned Paul, and dragged him out of the city, supposing that he was dead" (Acts 14:19). If you like the idea of receiving rewards due to persecution for Christ's namesake, take heart! Verbal persecution for not using a Christmas tree is nothing compared to being stoned, flogged, eaten by lions in the colosseum, beheaded, hung on a cross upside down, or jailed. What I mean is, you're doing okay if name-calling and an undesired reputation for being weird is all you have to endure! God sees you, and He is a rewarder of those who DILIGENTLY seek Him (Hebrews 11:6).

- CHAPTER 16 -

A WORLD OUTSIDE OF CHRISTMAS

My Christian friends, brothers and sisters, it was my blessed wife, Rachelle, who introduced these tough questions to me—tough questions for God's honor that fly boldly in the face of the world and its traditions, which are so thickly engrained in our culture today. At first, I pridefully and arrogantly blew it off, saying, "Don't mess with deep traditions that are filled with fun for everyone," but it was her boldness (not mine) that encouraged me to come back and take a real hard look at Christmas and how its lies have "conditioned" Christians to follow the crowd for so long.

As a result, following the crowd has never brought God's best for us, our country, or for mankind. I have been weak and wrong in many areas, but Rachelle has been such a solid example of how to search for things from a godly perspective: to diligently seek "everyday" situations with a perspective that consistently honors God.

It is my hope that the impact she has made on my heart transfers through this study into your hearts just the same and pays you spiritual dividends, too. This is what she calls "Secondary Blessings!"

Even though we just spent a good deal of time opening up and deeply examining the issue of Christmas for Christians, what I desire most through this book, is to effectively impart to you - a process. A process of challenging the hard questions.

Rachelle's willingness to stand up against all odds and question an overwhelmingly intimidating tradition is the influence I most want to share with you and ask that you emulate. I encourage you to take her example with you throughout the year everywhere and every day, not just during the Christmas holidays.

When you find yourself up against long-standing traditions, controversial issues, laws, policies, and even personal situations throughout your life, use this same process to discover the direction God desires for you. Don't be afraid to ask the question, "What does God say about this?"

Seek Him and listen for Him. Once you know God's stance, plant your feet and don't move!

Be blessed.

Thank you once again for reading

The Christian Christmas Condition.

Follow author Scott Rankin and be the first to know about upcoming early book releases, sneak peeks, FREE or DISCOUNTED deals, blog tour information, and other great BONUS materials!

Sign up here:

https://www.scottrankin.com/bonus

Want to be featured in Scott's follow up book?

In 750 words or less, submit your personal testimony of how *The Christian Christmas Condition* made an impact on you or your family. Your submission may be chosen as a feature in his follow up book!

https://www.scottrankin.com/submit-your-story

BIBLIOGRAPHY

"16 Types of Christmas Trees." *ProFlowers.com* November 15, 2018. <https://www.proflowers.com/blog/16-types-of-christmas-trees>.

Akin, Jimmy. "7 clues tell us precisely when Jesus died (the year, month, day, and hour revealed)." *National Catholic Register.* April 10, 2013. <http://www.ncregister.com/blog/jimmy-akin/when-precisely-did-jesus-die-the-year-month-day-and-hour-revealed>.

"Arguments For, and Against Christmas." *Theyouth4Christ Ministry.* December 26, 2011. <http://theyouthforjesus.blogspot.com/2011/12/arguments-for-and-against-christmas.html>.

"Asherah Semitic Goddess." *Encyclopaedia Britannica.* Editors of Encyclopaedia Britannica. September 10, 2019. <https://www.britannica.com/topic/Asherah-Semitic-goddess>.

"Baal Ancient Deity." *Encyclopaedia Britannica.* Editors of Encyclopaedia Britannica. August 12, 2019. <https://www.britannica.com/topic/Asherah-Semitic-goddess>.

Briggs, Jonathan. "Mistletoe Traditions." *The Mistletoe Pages.* January 2000. <http://mistletoe.org.uk/homewp/index.php/traditions/>.

"El Semitic Deity." *Encyclopaedia Britannica.* Editors of Encyclopaedia Britannica. September 10, 2019. <https://www.britannica.com/topic/Asherah-Semitic-goddess>.

Friel, Todd. "What Should We Do About Christmas?" *Wretched.* December 22, 2014. February 5, 2018. <https://www.youtube.com/watch?v=FzuZB7OGoZ4>.

Hill, Jenny. "Ra." *Ancient Egypt Online.* 2008. September 10, 2019. <https://ancientegyptonline.co.uk/ra/>.

Hillerbrand, Hans J. "Christmas Holiday." *Encyclopaedia Britannica.* Editors of Encyclopaedia Britannica. July 20, 1998. <https://www.britannica.com/topic/Christmas>.

Handwerk, Brian. "From St. Nicholas to Santa Claus: the surprising origins of Kris Kringle." *National Geographic.* December 20, 2013. December 25, 2018. <https://www.nationalgeographic.com/news/2018/12/131219-santa-claus-origin-history-christmas-facts-st-nicholas/>.

History.com Editors. "History of Christmas." *A&E Television Networks.* October 27, 2009. February 7, 2019. <https://www.history.com/topics/christmas/history-of-christmas>.

History.com Editors. "History of Christmas Trees." *A&E Television Networks.* October 27, 2009. September 12, 2018. <https://www.history.com/topics/christmas/history-of-christmas-trees>.

History.com Editors. "Santa Claus." *A&E Television Networks.* February 16, 2010. December 6, 2018. <https://www.history.com/topics/christmas/santa-claus>.

History.com Editors. "Saturnalia." *HISTORY*. September 10, 2019. <https://www.history.com/topics/ancient-rome/saturnalia>.

The Holy Bible, World English Bible (WEB). Public Domain.

"Kirk Cameron – Liberty University Convocation." September 30, 2014. <https://www.youtube.com/watch?v=mPJA8hn6tLY>.

Klein, Christopher. "When Massachusetts Banned Christmas." *History.com.* December 22, 2015. September 1, 2018. <https://www.history.com/news/when-massachusetts-banned-christmas>.

Lipsman, Andrew. "US 2018 Holiday Season Review and 2019 Preview." *eMarketer*. February 21, 2019. <https://www.emarketer.com/content/us-2018-holiday-season-review-and-2019-preview>.

Mark, Joshua J. "Thor." *Ancient History Encyclopedia*. December 17, 2018. <https://www.ancient.eu/Thor/>.

McGowan, Andrew. "How December 25 Became Christmas." *Biblical Archaeology Society*. December 2002. December 25, 2018. <https://www.biblicalarchaeology.org/daily/people-cultures-in-the-bible/jesus-historical-jesus/how-december-25-became-christmas/>.

New World Encyclopedia contributors. "Bibliographic Details for Canaanite Religion." *New World Encyclopedia*. March 8, 2019. <https://www.newworldencyclopedia.org/p/index.php?title=Canaanite_Religion&oldid=1018918>.

New World Encyclopedia contributors. "Thor." *New World Encyclopedia*. December 7, 2015. <https://www.newworldencyclopedia.org/entry/Thor>.

Pack, David C. "The True Origin of Christmas." *The Real Truth*. September 11, 2019. <https://rcg.org/realtruth/articles/169-ttooc.html>.

Pruitt, Sarah. "Why is Christmas celebrated on December 25th?" *History.com*. December 24, 2012. August 31, 2018. <https://www.history.com/news/why-is-christmas-celebrated-on-december-25>.

Rhodes, Ron, PhD. "How Did Lucifer Fall and Become Satan?" *Christianity.com*. October 22, 2007. February 5, 2018. <https://www.christianity.com/theology/theological-faq/how-did-lucifer-fall-and-become-satan-11557519.html>.

"Saturnalia Roman Festival." *Encyclopaedia Britannica*. Editors of Encyclopaedia Britannica. March 3, 2017. <https://www.britannica.com/topic/Saturnalia-Roman-festival>.

Sewell, Matthew. "Thor, St. Boniface, and the Origin of the Christmas Tree." *Mountain Catholic*. December 23, 2014. <https://mtncatholic.com/2014/12/23/thor-stboniface-and-the-origin-of-the-christmas-tree/>.

"Tertullian." *Christianity.com*. September 11, 2019. <https://www.christianity.com/church/church-history/timeline/1-300/tertullian-11629598.html>.

Thiel, Bob, PhD. "Did Early Christians Celebrate Birthdays?" *COGWRITER*. September 11, 2019. <https://www.cogwriter.com/birthdays.htm>.

"Thor Germanic Deity." *Encyclopaedia Britannica*. Editors of Encyclopaedia Britannica. August 10, 2019. <https://www.britannica.com/topic/Thor-Germanic-deity>.

Waxman, Olivia B. "The True History of St. Nicholas is a Christmas Mystery." *Time.com*. December 22, 2017. <https://time.com/5068085/st-nicholas-santa-history/>.

Weidenkopf, Steve. "St. Boniface and the Christmas Tree." *Catholic Answers*. June 5, 2014. <https://www.catholic.com/magazine/online-edition/st-boniface-and-the-christmas-tree>.

"What is an Asherah Pole?" *www.gotquestions.org*. July 26, 2019. <https://www.gotquestions.org/Asherah-pole.html>.

Printed in Great Britain
by Amazon